The Parker Ranch of Hawaii

Joseph Brennan

The Parker Ranch
of Hawaii

The Saga of a Ranch

and a Dynasty

The
John
Day
Company

An Intext Publisher · New York

The John Day Company, 257 Park Avenue South, New York, N.Y. 10010.
Published on the same day in Canada by Longman Canada Limited.
Printed in the United States of America.

Library of Congress Cataloging in Publication Data

Brennan, Joseph.
  The Parker Ranch of Hawaii; the saga of a ranch and
a dynasty.

  1. Parker Ranch, Hawaii. 2. Parker family.
3. Hawaii—History. I. Title.
DU629.P3B73 1974   929'.2'0973   73–18537
ISBN   0–381–98265–3

To Harriet "Blondie" Brennan

Contents

Illustrations

Colonel Sam Parker's home at Kawaihae

The old-time *paniolos* on the range

Paniolos transferring cattle from beach to freighter, through the surf at Kawaihae

Elizabeth Jane Dowsett Parker (Aunt Tootsie)

John Palmer Parker III

Alfred Wellington Carter

Aunt Tootsie

Thelma Parker

Annie Thelma Parker Smart as a bride

Henry Gaillard Smart, on the grounds at Puuopelu

Thelma Parker Smart and her son Richard

Aunt Tootsie and young Richard

Richard Palmer Smart

Snow-covered Mount Mauna Kea, as seen from the Parker Ranch

Paniolos, and the remnants of volcanic cones on the Ranch land

Introduction

When the Second World War came to a conclusion and these small Hawaiian Islands of the Pacific gradually returned to normal, I developed a wish that some of the past could be recorded. In looking over Parker Ranch as I sat in my office, I could dream out the window and think about early days of past generations. Imagining the broad forests which no longer exist, I wished to preserve what it was like in those early days—how the people reacted to the problems of the pioneer—what it was like when wild cattle roamed the plains and the vigorous and strong *paniolo*, or cowboy, suffered many hardships.

The forties passed and the fifties, but no one had come along to be the historian of this area. One bright morning there was a call from Joseph Brennan, who told me, in a few words, that he wanted to write the history of the Parker Ranch and its people. I was impressed and happy that someone had finally arrived with the interest, the desire, and the background of living in Hawaii which would make my dream a reality.

The association with Joseph Brennan started by correspondence, and I began feeding him as much information as possible collected from the files. Numerous old letters were at his disposal. Joe started in earnest to research the entire subject. Over a period of several months, each time I traveled to Honolulu on business I would spend a few hours with Joe. These were truly exhilarating experiences. Whenever we got together he had pages of questions to fire at me, and I tried my best to answer them. Our discussions usually turned to reminiscenses which helped to fill in the gaps of this Hawaiian saga.

As the work progressed through several years, Joe's first feeling that the end of the book should constantly be kept contemporary changed, for as in any book, there has to be an end, and I think he closed it wisely. Parker Ranch will go on, and next year will be different from this year, but many exciting years lie in the past of the last century and up to the 1970s.

This book shows a sincere, true, and authentic picture of the times that it chronicles. It has successfully captured the life and times of the early settlers in the annals of Hawaiian history. One realizes that the Wild West extends farther than Texas, Arizona, and New Mexico and that a part of it has existed for many years in the middle of the Pacific. Hawaii, our fiftieth state, has many facets, and on its mountainous slopes we find the trade winds nurturing a strong and vigorous land, developed by rugged individualists.

RICHARD SMART

The Parker Ranch
October 30, 1973

Preface

A definitive history of a ranch, a person, what-have-you, is almost an anachronism in these blasé, sex-obsessed, violent, revolutionary days. But we here document the story of a vast legendary cattle ranch which is an integral part of the history of Hawaii, and should, we think, be told. The land itself is rare, beautiful, and awe-inspiring. The history of how the ranch was founded and developed into the modern cattle dynasty that it is today beggars fiction.

The men and women of the Parker Ranch were exceptional; they still are today. The fabulous and venturesome John Palmer Parker founded the ranch, and put his mark upon the land for all time. His wife and the mother of his children, a granddaughter of King Kamehameha the Great, proved fit mate for him and fought valiantly at his side through their darkest years. Other strong, dedicated men and women followed him, but he was the bellwether of the lot. Ebenezer and John, his sons, came after him, both of them of the same qualities. The first died too young to have reached and demonstrated his full potential. The other lived for sixty-four years —most of them productive ones. But after them, the grandson Samuel Parker preferred to live as the colorful playboy of the line.

Along with these persons were others who made the Parker Ranch what it was and is today. Too much credit cannot be given to Elizabeth Jane Lanakila Dowsett Parker, better known as "Aunt

Tootsie." She was the outstanding woman who married John Parker III, the son of Sam Parker. It was her good judgment and faith that once again guided a cattle empire that had started to falter badly. She delegated the astute Alfred Wellington Carter to manage the vast estate which John Parker the patriarch had left to his heirs. Carter managed the ranch from 1899 through long stormy years, and without him the whole cattle empire might well have decayed and disintegrated.

Carter and the men under him perpetuated the spirit which had first been instilled into the ranch by the first John Parker. Carter selected quality men for the key jobs and sweated and planned with them for a whole lifetime. The result was a thriving cattle dynasty operated by individuals who had the very breath of John Parker in their souls. Such a kingdom in such an exotic land as Hawaii deserved a long line of outstanding people. Their trials, tribulations, and successes are the grist of this book. It is hoped that this will in some way immortalize a few of them.

I have reported the facts here as I have found them, checked, and double-checked them, and all the while striven not to be doggedly chronological, which could well prove deadly dull. If the document lacks the texture of life, it is due to the author's deficiencies—not to those men who rode so tall in the saddle for so long.

Acknowledgments

The author wishes to thank the following people and acknowledge useful sources for generous help in the preparation of this book:

The late Mary Low and her many handwritten letters to Richard Smart during 1931, 1932, and 1933, giving much genealogy, ranch history, and many personal experiences of her own during the many years when she lived on the Parker Ranch as a member of the family; the files of the Hawaii State Library System; the files and archives of the University of Hawaii Library and its Hawaiian and Pacific Room, with particular assistance from Miss Janet Bell, Head Librarian; the *Hawaiian Historical Society Annual Reports*; scores of old and new issues from the *Honolulu Star Bulletin;* back copies of the *Honolulu Advertiser;* the Hawaii State Archives; *Hawaii of Today,* by Lieut. R. C. Wriston, A.A. USA (Doubleday, 1926); Larry Kimura's "Old-time Parker Ranch Cowboys" (*Hawaii Historical Review*, 1964); Clifford Gessler's "Hawaii: Isles of Enchantment"; Volumes I, II, and III of Captain George Vancouver's diary *A Voyage of Discovery to the North Pacific Ocean and Round the World,* N. Israel, Amsterdam Da Capo Press, New York 1967; "The Story of Alfred Wellington Carter, 1867–1949," by Emma Lyons Doyle; the Parker Ranch monthly house organ, issues from initial printing December 1961 to August 1970, inclusive; Mr. Richard Smart; Mr. Hartwell Carter; the management of *Paradise of the Pacific* magazine.

The Parker Ranch of Hawaii

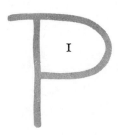
I

Big and Splendid

ARKER RANCH! There is an eerie, lingering silence about this ancient Hawaiian region, a sense of something waiting; there is something about the quiet—a feeling that the ghosts, bronzed, barefooted Polynesians are padding past you, even though you can't see them. You look out over Parker land, and your thoughts merge with sun-drenched grass, quiet forest, porcelain-blue sky, and the distant lyric sea.

Those primitives who peopled this vast place are now gone, leaving only loneliness behind. You wish you could somehow roll back the veil of time and see the people themselves. The mountains and hills are majestic, the sky virgin, the air tonic. The springtime plain is carpeted with brilliant, fragile blossoms. In winter the high-piled clouds trail their screens of rain across to polished land. All of it looks as timeless as the planets —and as you look, your thoughts turn toward the past, and you wonder about those people who called it home.

You gaze at this cattle ranch from high on the misty heights of Hawaii's Mauna Kea, and from the volcano's sloping shoulder you see 227,000 acres, a breathtaking vista spread out on the highlands of this great mountain. A soothing wind drifts from the mountain and cools the lava wastes. Seemingly limitless, the area includes forests, valleys, seashore, plateaus, meadows, hills, streams, and canyons. This is the sprawling, mysterious, majestic Parker Ranch, with the largest Hereford herd in the world.

The three huge parcels of land making up this ranch are so divergent in their swaths of acreage across the face of North Hawaii that its annual rainfall varies from six inches to more than 100 inches. One can conceive of its incredible makeup and size when considering that one can drive from hot, flat prairie to high mountain or deep canyons thick with ti, lehua, banana, and tree fern.

Much of this cattle world is high on Mauna Kea's bare volcanic slopes; much of it is low, grassy plain; much of it is mountain steepness with the natural peaks, valleys, canyons, and meadows. You can experience many kinds of weather and precipitation by moving from one part of the ranch to another. In the lower regions the weather is mostly "postcard perfect"; a winter cold snap leaves the top of Mauna Kea bundled in ermine.

Today all of this ranch's fantastic land—range, forest, and seacoast—is owned and operated by Richard Palmer Kaleioku Smart, the sixth-generation heir of founder John Palmer Parker. It has been a continuous family operation for 136 years. Smart's domain extends from the cloud-washed slopes of the extinct volcano to the ocean. One can scan it with the heady knowledge that it is still the largest cattle ranch under single ownership in the United States (its competitor, the King Ranch of Texas, is a corporation holding).

Over 51,000 head of the world's finest Herefords range the land. The flow and turn of cattle herds here seems as endless as the tides. More than 1,000 horses, mostly thoroughbreds, are on the hoof here as a part of the working assembly of the spread. There are 132 people on the Parker Ranch payroll, and long ago it was arranged for one-fourth of the ranch's net income to go to the benefit of its employees. That still holds, thanks to Mr. Richard Smart.

Some 600 miles of fencing embraces this acreage, to say nothing of the long shorelines which serve the same purpose. The ranch's 200 water tanks, 210 water troughs, and 170 ground tanks are supplied by over 160 miles of pipeline. The average rancher's mind boggles at the figures of 213 paddocks, 50 corrals, 207 houses and buildings—along with the army of tractors, trucks, and other vehicles which service the Parker layout.

But once one knows all the facts about this island ranch, it isn't the fantastic acreage that captures the imagination so much as the history of the founder and his descendants who have made it what it is. Theirs is the heart of the story—a story of people who played their part in the saga of this cattle empire.

The heartbeat of the story of the Parker Ranch is a history of people—people like John Palmer Parker who founded a monumental dynasty. It is a story of heroic proportions. His living heir today, Richard Smart, will put no monetary value upon the property. A Texas syndicate once offered to buy it from him and suggested that he name his own price. He replied with honesty: "There is no price." He meant it.

One senses high adventure on every acre of the spread. Excitement permeates its very paddocks, stables, pastures, buildings, and homes. High spirit is part of the nature of those who live here and belong here. It is part of the fabric of the unity and pattern and rhythm which Parker Ranch people feel. Some wear it like a badge—pridefully—and they like to talk about it. Some wear it secretly in their hearts—and never put it into words. But deep down inside, their pride is just as great, and their allegiance is unfettered.

All this accounts for a pace, a tempo, for the hard-riding *paniolos*, the Hawaiian cowboys who have the chores of herding, cutting, holding, roping, throwing, branding, castrating, inoculating, ear-clipping, medicating, sorting, loading, and shipping the ever moving, bellowing animals.

Where else can you find a view quite like the bulky rolling hills and mountain slopes that appear to be sliding away from majestic Mauna Kea? Its beauty is breathtaking. Deep-forested canyons slice in between, flat grass-grown prairie stretches below, and limitless blue ocean spreads beyond. The sound of centuries is in its surf and is carried on the wind.

One scans the far-flung range and sees an undulating herd of cattle moving slowly like a red swollen river. The moving figures at the edges are mounted *paniolos* urging the animals along. Dust rises from the sun-drenched earth. There is a soft, distant bellowing from the herd, and an occasional deep-throated shout from one or more of the horsemen. This is Parker Ranch on the move, animated Parker Ranch with its fabulous history, its high spirit of adventure and progress, and its promise of even better things tomorrow. It has a look, a sound, a fragrance, and a feel of all the good things that are happening and will happen here. This immense spread of land, with the ancient, long-dead volcano towering over it, was the cradle of cattle ranching in Hawaii.

An excellent lady journalist, Lois Stewart, once described this magnificent spread which John Parker founded. Beautifully and artfully, she said in part in the Honolulu *Advertiser:*

> What is Parker Ranch, outside of its vastness?
> It is a village, it is canyons, paddocks, meadows and valleys.
> It is crags and the crash of surf on beautiful beach.
> It is Mana, the first home of the Parkers.
> It is gracious Puuopelu, the century-old home of Richard Smart.
> It is a drift of geraniums, and the staccato of hooves, the bleat of calves, and the sad, sweet melody of the wind in a lonely burial ground.

Hardships were the lot of the Parkers and their kin, but from John Parker himself down to the present owner, they met reverses and challenges head on and won against odds that would have turned back many a stout man. The so-called Parker kingdom has become more than a cattle ranch; it has become an institution, an ideal, a way of life.

It all began with old John Palmer Parker back in the mid-1800s; he had a dream, held it close to him, and made it come true. A cattle dynasty was born. He went on developing it with enormous vigor and imagination. He made a religion of self-reliance—and it paid off hugely.

Long after the patriarch's demise in 1868, Alfred Carter came into the breach in 1899 when the ranch was in decline. Because of his dynamic and studied ways, the ranch once more began prospering and growing. These two men, in their own times, made the ranch come alive. Theirs was a blend of talent that pioneered a basic industry for the Hawaiian Islands.

The Parker Ranch story is basically the tale of men—men and the strong, heroic women who backed them to the hilt. What they received in return—wages, rations, housing—they knew it to be but a part of the result of their efforts, an integral part in the progress and success of the whole—the Parker Ranch.

Times of the Polynesians

THIS COUNTRY, which holds the Parker Ranch in its wide arms, is legendary for the Polynesian kings, queens, chiefs, and chieftesses who have trod its length and breadth. Hordes of brave warriors have fought and died here. Below the *alii* (royal) and priestly class were the *makaainana* (commoners), who made their homes in the region for centuries. There was a third class of people, the *kauwa*—those who had broken the taboos or were despised for other reasons. They had no property rights and lived as outcasts, peopling some of the area and doing the *alii's* bidding.

To those who know the region, it is additionally colorful and historic because they realize that in the middle of the 1700s, during King Alapainui's reign, Kamehameha I was born at Halawa in North Kohala. They also know the story of how the infant was carried across these lands up into Waipio Valley in North Kohala and concealed from the executioners sent out by King Alapainui.

It should be pointed out that in those times each island usually had one *alii nui*, or *moi* (king), who was the most powerful of the *alii*. King Alapainui happened to be *alii nui* on Hawaii at the time. The infant's mother was High Chieftess Kekuiapoiwa, niece of the king of Hawaii, and her husband was High Chief Keoua—all of them members of the *alii-kapu*, or sacred rulers.

6

King Alapainui of Hawaii was an uncle of High Chief Keoua, the husband of the baby's mother, and the king feared that this child might someday have a following of his own and come into power on the island. Even King Alapainui's *kahunas*, or priests, had prophesied that the infant would become a renegade and a destroyer of chiefs. Alarmed, Alapainui decreed, "The child must die!"

All this was in the fall of 1758, and it accounts for a powerful native, High Chief Naeole, pushing through a wild night of lashing wind, lightning, and booming thunder below the slopes of snow-capped Mauna Kea. In his arms he carried the newborn tapa-covered baby.

At the birth of this coppery-skinned infant, a fiery comet burned its way across the western firmament as though in tribute to the first day on earth of this great king-to-be. That glowing ball with a fiery tail has since become known as Halley's comet, and it has helped historians to determine the year of the infant's birth.

History was in the making. No land needed a single, strong leader as much as did this archipelago, for, as pointed out, the several inhabited islands had their own kings, their own chiefs and their own underchiefs, who were constantly warring against each other on a one-way road to self-extinction. Their wars were brutal and pagan. To understand those ancient times, it is necessary to know that the people worshiped many gods. Each man had his own *akua*, the god that was believed to watch over him personally. The man made an image of wood or wickerwork or feathers to represent the god, and he fully believed that the spirits of the god lived within this crude creation.

The region through which Naeole pushed two-hundred years ago was the same rough, tangled terrain that it is today. Naeole struggled through cascades of wild morning glory vines, pushed among dense *kamani* trees, and threaded groves of *halas*, or "walking trees," bordering the taro patches.

The little grass house at Halawa where the infant had been

born was left farther and farther behind. Naeole knew that King Alapainui's men were due there at any instant, and their dismay at not finding the newborn babe would lead to a thorough combing of the countryside.

The rain- and sweat-soaked runner slogged and panted those last few mountain miles above Waipio Valley and finally reached the planned hideout, a cave forming part of a lava tube which led into the recesses of the hillside. At the entrance a native priest and several friends of the child's royal mother waited, tense and anxious. Naeole stumbled into the group, and quickly, quietly, they took the small bundle of human life from him, tended carefully to it, and turned it over to the care of another native mother. Meanwhile, the priest performed religious rites over the child, blessing it, and praying for it.

In the gray hours of the morning, some of the king's spearmen were combing the area. Those in the cave spoke in whispers. The wrath of the searchers was great when these temporary dwellers of the cave were finally located by them. But the infant had already been hidden deeper in the recesses of the lava tube. The natives told the armed men that they knew of no newborn babe in the region. The king's warriors only intensified their search. Their own lives would be at stake if they did not find and kill the infant. But the black hideaway kept its secret, and the would-be executioners departed.

The cave with its child of royal blood was guarded day and night. Occasionally runners got through to Kekuiapoiwa to advise her of the safety and progress of her son. From time to time she sent back instructions on the care and training of her firstborn. For about a month this hideout was maintained, then upon the High Chieftess' orders, the baby was taken down the mountain trails deep into the beautiful valley of Waipio. Again it was the loyal and dedicated Naeole who carried the child.

With the summit of towering Mauna Kea lost in the clouds to the southeast, this long gorge lay landlocked by ranges and cliffs. Hardly reachable, except by sea, the hidden valley offered almost as secure a hideout as the cave had furnished. It was a lush place for the boy to grow up in; its little grass houses clustered here and there at the foot of the mountains were a picture of peace and serenity. Waterfalls and springs supplied the bottomland with year-round irrigation. The rich soil made the taro crops a thing to behold. Coconut palms forested much of the flatland, and banana groves and thickets of immense breadfruit trees spread in every direction.

Before this land became cattle country, much warfare took place. Polynesian blood stained its soil and ran in rivulets on its lava beds. The Waimea plains, the seat of today's Parker Ranch, saw fighting as ferocious and bloody as any hostilities that ever took place throughout the Islands. In the time of King Lonoikamakahiki, the great monarch of the Island of Hawaii before King Kamehameha's time (c. 1758–1819), Maui forces came over in great armadas and tried to subdue the island. The combat forces were led by Maui's King Kamalalawalu and were backed by an enormous fleet of war canoes loaded with warriors. It was a frightful battle, beginning on the seacoast from Anae-hoomalu to Puako, and onto the plains of Waimea where the heaviest fighting developed. After much bloodshed, with combat seesawing one way and then the other, the king of Hawaii's forces were victorious over the Mauians, who were completely routed.

In the 1780s, with King Alapainui long dead and King Kalaniopuu now the monarch at Kona, new resistance and insurrection were taking place in the districts of Kau and Puna. Young Kamehameha had proved himself such an adept warrior in the king's army that he had been made an aide to the monarch, and was now part of the royal court. Due to constant warring, the resources at Kona had been acutely drained, and Kalaniopuu moved his entire court northward to the district of Kohala. So, once again Kamehameha was in the land of his birth—the region where he was fostered and trained as a child.

Time went by, but serenity was not to last. In the south Chief Imakakoloa and his warriors resumed pressing the civil war. They struck hard. The attacks roused old King Kalaniopuu from his languor, and he prepared to strike back. He took Kamehameha with him and went to the southern part of his kingdom to suppress the rapidly growing revolt. He not only defeated the opposing forces, but he captured the rebel chieftain and took him to the *heiau* (temple, pronounced *hay-ee-ow*) of Pakini in Kau to be sacrificed to the war god.

The ghastly ceremony—the sacrifice of Chief Imakakoloa—furnished the occasion for Kamehameha's first open resistance to the court. King Kalaniopuu's son, Chief Kiwalao, was at the altar in the midst of rituals preliminary to the actual human sacrifice when Kamehameha stepped in and took over the rite himself.

"It is my right," he said, "as custodian of the war god Kukailimoku!"

Some chiefs froze in their tracks; others voiced their astonishment at this act of aggressiveness. Kiwalao protested loudly and angrily, but King Kalaniopuu shouted, "So be it! Kamehameha is right!" Kiwalao backed down, and thus there was more bad blood between him and Kamehameha.

After the ceremonies, King Kalaniopuu took a prudent step to avoid more court conflict. He sent Kamehameha back up to Halawa in the Kohala district, where young Kamehameha remained with his wife, Kalola, his brother, Kalaimamahu, and his own retainers who made up his own court.

Kamehameha was at the zenith of his young manhood at this time. He was almost six and a half feet tall and in robust health. His body had the heavy-boned and barrel-chested proportions of a sleek, muscular show horse. His hair was black and shiny as rain-wet lava, and his skin was the rich color of coffee that has been slightly creamed. Kamehameha had a carriage and a stance that only heightened the beauty of his body. It has been said by historians and old-time sailing men who saw him that he had a fierce, savage face, but there are those who insist it was merely the lonely look of a withdrawn and grave man. His deep-set black eyes were changeable, burning sometimes with an inner zeal, sometimes with a certain mourning. His voice was a rich baritone.

Too, Kamehameha was held in high favor by people over whom he now had jurisdiction in the districts of Kohala, Kona, and Hamakua. The people of Waipio Valley were particularly elated over his assignment to the northern region because of their early childhood kinship with him.

Old King Kalaniopuu named his son Kiwalao to be heir after him. He made Kamehameha next in line for the throne. Then the death of Kalaniopuu in 1782 was followed by civil war on the Big Island, with Kamehameha striving to attain the monarchy. At a battle near the City of Refuge, Kiwalao was killed, and Kamehameha took full jurisdiction over all Kona.

In Halawa, Kamehameha had, in a sense, been in exile, but it had not kept the rising young chief from showing his ability as an organizer, a builder, and a leader. He ruled with an iron hand, but, in truth, when he willed it, his charm was immense.

He worked with his people at cultivating and improving the land and at constructing a fleet of canoes for fishing and for war. He assisted in building fishponds and constructing dams and irrigation canals. This was quite a switch among rulers and subrulers, for he did these things with an eye to the future. He obviously was not thinking only in terms of present needs and wants, but in terms of years to come when a new generation of people would profit by these labors. He wanted no part of war or strife.

There was no room for laziness in Kamehameha's scheme of things. No man could long remain apathetic in the presence of this chief. Among other ambitious developments, Kamehameha had a mammoth wall of stone, six feet high and twenty feet wide, erected across a half-mile bay to serve as a fishpond. It encircled a two-mile area and assured his people of fish when the catch was not good. Kamehameha threw his lot in with the people of the north, showed them the dignity of honest labor by working and sweating at their side. Breaking soil, moving rocks, hauling nets—none of these mundane chores was beneath him. He knew the integrity of heavy, sweaty toil. Today the descendants of those people of North Hawaii still revere the name of Kamehameha.

But he did suffer defeats. One place in Parker Ranch country which still marks one of Kamehameha's worst defeats is Kawaihae. He was warring with self-styled kings Keawemauhili and Keoua, and attempted his now famous *Kama-ino* expedition where his warriors crossed the mountains ranging down from the north. To fortify his attack, he put all his war canoe strength under the command of Chief Keeaumoku in the Bay of Kawaihae—today's shipping point for all Parker Ranch cattle. The instructions were for the chief to take the flotilla on around the north tip of Hawaii and make for Hilo on the east. It was Kamehameha's intent to keep apart the warriors of Keawemauhili and Keoua, defeat them separately, then march to the flotilla of canoes waiting at Hilo and consolidate there.

However, it did not work out that way. At the start, the wind picked up, and it began to rain. Flashes of lightning washed across the southern sky. It seemed an ill omen, and Kamehameha's men were grim and dismayed. He and his warriors suffered during the long, painful trek across the stark, lava-strewn mountains, through the cold rain. They were in bad shape when they encountered Keawemauhili's army in Puna.

Under a sky of aluminum-colored clouds, Kamehameha and his men fought valiantly, but they were beaten. The presence of the squadron of war canoes at Hilo was the only thing that saved his ranks from being decimated. Today old-timers still point at the harbor at Kawaihae and tell of the proud sailing from that port—and the havoc which Kamehameha's legions encountered. The flotilla served more as an ambulance corps than as an attacking force. The defeated army returned under soggy, gloomy, cloud-scudding rain.

Kawaihae is also historic for another great clash of arms in 1790. The previous years had been characterized by intermittent periods of vicious combat in various regions of the Big Island. All three chiefs were vying for power. Keoua finally went on the warpath and invaded Hilo in a heavy assault of his own. His attack on Keawemauhili's forces was successful, for the latter's Puna warriors were battered and beaten unmercifully. Chief Keawemauhili was slain in the invasion, and the district was taken over by Keoua and his army.

Immediately upon adding all of Puna to his own kingdom of Kau, Keoua turned his assault to Kamehameha's northern districts. He attacked and ransacked Waipio, Hamakua, and Waimea, practicing something like "scorched-earth" warfare. Keoua's legions slaughtered pigs, burned huts, poisoned the fishponds, and destroyed crops, particularly the important fields of taro.

In the fall of 1790 Kamehameha assembled his armada of warriors at Kawaihae and engaged the Keoua marauders in force at that point. It was a heroic stand, so much so that Kamehameha and his legions drove Keoua to the other side of the island at Paauhau, where the two armies fought to a standstill, neither being able to gain an advantage. The losses were frightful, and both sides left the battlefield battered and shrunken. Keoua and his warriors returned to Hilo, and Kamehameha retreated to Kohala. This was rapidly developing into a war of extinction—almost genocide—so both sides took time out to regroup themselves and replenish.

Keoua divided his newly won Puna lands among his under-chiefs, then accompanied his warriors on the long trek home to

Kau. Unexpectedly, a volcanic eruption took a further toll of his men on the slopes of Kilauea. It was many days before he and what was left of his army reached home. Far to the rear of them on the fiery lava flows lay many scalded, scorched corpses.

The respite continued into 1791, both armies licking their wounds in their own respective districts. In the north, Kamehameha continued showing his great capacity for organization, for governing, and for listening. He talked to many wise old *kahunas*, asking them for advice on how he could defeat Keoua-of-the-Flaming-Cloak, who had brought him to disaster.

From a renowned soothsayer of Kauai, Kamehameha learned that he should build a large temple for his war god, Kukailimoku. In addition, he was told to sacrifice the body of an enemy chief on its altar. Kamehameha proceeded to build the *heiau*, or temple, at once on the slopes of Kawaihae Bay. Puukohola would be the name of the temple, and vast armies of men toiled in relays to complete the gigantic edifice. Kamehameha didn't spare the chiefs nor himself; he and his chiefs worked and strained shoulder to shoulder along with the commoners. Thousands upon thousands of workers camped on the surrounding hillsides and beaches during this operation. It was a project of hand labor, massive and high, and all the people and chiefs from Kona, Kohala, and Hamakua assisted in its building. Tens of thousands of stones were passed hand-to-hand from distant Kohala lands.

However, after the Puukohola *heiau* was well under construction, a stunning interruption hit Kamehameha and his throngs of workers. It was war again, and this time where and when he least expected it. King Kahekili of the island of Oahu had combined his forces with those of Kaeokulani, king of Kauai, and the two of them had sailed their armada of war canoes southeastward and taken over Molokai and Maui. Next they took their flotilla of warriors across the waters to the northern coast of Hawaii, struck hard, and ravished the land and the people.

It was a surprise attack against his own kingdom, and Kamehameha had been caught off guard. He halted his building of the *heiau* and marshaled his forces to hit back at the invaders. Hurriedly, he assembled a large fleet, including double canoes mounted with swivel guns under the supervision of two *haoles* (foreigners), Isaac Davis and John Young. He struck and struck hard.

Kamehameha's forces collided in heavy combat with the invaders off Waipio. With the leeward rulers' canoes also equipped with firearms, and foreigners in charge of them, it was a new kind of maritime war for the natives. The two fleets fought a long, bloody battle. It was civil war all over again, with Polynesians slaughtering Polynesians.

The battle had begun shortly after midday, and not until sundown did Kamehameha's heavier bombardment and hand-to-hand defense prove adequate to win the fight. He drove off the invaders and stampeded them back to their own waters. The battle was later to be known as Kepuwahaulaula—"the red-mouthed gun."

Returning battered but victorious to his fleet's home waters, Kamehameha lost no time in turning his mind and time to further erection of the temple at Kawaihae Bay. There would be time enough to attack Oahu and Maui to retaliate for this treacherous raid. Too, with his victory, there seemed all the more reason for erecting the *heiau* to his war god, Kukailimoku. After many more weeks of sweat and labor, the sacred structure was completed and ready for dedication. It was late summer of 1791 now and time for great rejoicing. Commoners and royalty alike celebrated the completion of the new temple. It was a magnificent edifice—224 feet long, 100 feet wide, with walls twelve feet high. New images of the gods were carved and placed in proper wall niches and atop pedestals.

Amid the most ceremonious fanfare—and with only those of highest blood looking on—the high priest carried Kukailimoku, Kamehameha's war-god image in a closely woven wicker basket and placed it in the niche prepared for it. Guttural chanting and rhythmic beating of sharkskin drums accompanied the procession. And now the sacred temple was ready for the sacrificial offering of a chief's body. But whose body? What chief? Kamehameha's enemy to the south, Keoua?

At this juncture an unexplained historical point comes up. Kamehameha's court had invited Keoua of Kau to come to Kawaihae to help work out a plan for peace. In fact, the two great chiefs, Keaweaheulu and Kamanawa, who had supported Kamehameha so loyally for nine years were the ambassadors who took the invitation to Keoua. The latter accepted.

Keoua and his highest chiefs arrived at Kawaihae Bay in a brace of canoes, one commanded by himself, and the other by a young man named Kaoleioku. The sight of the new temple gracing the green slope above Kawaihae Bay was impressive, and Keoua could not help but be further convinced that Kamehameha was ambitious and had a tremendous hold upon the people, the chiefs, and the priests. Standing in the canoe, the sun on his bright feather helmet and cloak, Keoua was every inch a king himself in appearance—but it is said that he clearly had evil premonitions of what might happen.

History reports that Keoua Kuahuula said to his men in his canoe, "The flight of the clouds is ominous ashore." Hesitantly, he studied the scene further and saw Kamehameha standing on the beach in his golden-feathered cloak and helmet. High Chief Keeaumoku, the prime minister, stood not far away with additional armed warriors.

Keoua called to Kamehameha, "Here I am!"

Kamehameha called back, "Rise and come up that we may know each other!"

Keoua jumped ashore as the canoe touched the bank. In this instant, with no warning whatsoever, Keeaumoku hurled a spear straight into the body of Keoua and killed him outright. At least, these are supposed to be the bare facts. With no written language among the early Hawaiians, we have to rely upon their *meles* and chants passed on down from mouth to mouth over the years.

Immediately, violent fighting broke out at the shore's edge. It was a pitched battle, wholly unequal as to numbers on a side. Every warrior of the first canoe save one was speedily massacred. Those in the second canoe, too, would have suffered the same ruthless slaughter had not Kamehameha ordered his men to spare them. He had recognized the young man in command as his own son, Kaoleioku, whom he had fathered so many years ago in Kau. The boy had all the beauty and grace of his mother, the High Chieftess Kanekapolei, and Kamehameha wanted no harm to come to him.

Partisan friends of Kamehameha's have since insisted that this treacherous incident was devised and triggered solely by the opportunist, Keeaumoku, who wanted nothing to stand in the way of Kamehameha's reign as king. History tells us that the corpse of Keoua-of-the-Flaming-Cloak was offered up on the altar as sacrifice to the war god Kukailimoku. Ten additional human beings were also immolated.

Now Kamehameha was absolute ruler of all on the Big Island. He had the support of most of the people of Kau, who remembered the "Lonely One" when he had been but a young man in their midst. Even those who counted the Kawaihae Bay incident a thing of outright treachery now had to bow down to the new regime.

To his court, Kamehameha announced in his stentorian voice, "I now take the title of *Moi* (King)!" King he was, too, for no one could now gainsay him the right to rule. He had won his war for the Big Island.

And so to this day the very name of Kawaihae is synonymous with Kamehameha, for the great king who united the Islands in years to come, spent much of his youth and adulthood in this northern region. He fought some of his decisive battles here, and his building of the *heiau* at Kawaihae put his mark upon the land. With him as their leader, the commoners took a stronger grip on the threads of life. The future wouldn't be peaceful, but at least civil war was back of them—civil war, that is, on the Big Island.

Somehow the fact that ancient Polynesians built some of their *heiaus* on and near what is today's Parker Ranch lends an additional luster, color, and romanticism to the whole region. So much that lies shrouded in the mists of ancient years happened on Parker land.

One might at first discount the Polynesian importance of these temples. But one temple alone—the Wahaula *heiau* in Puna—was one of rigid *kapus* (taboos), scene of the most cruel of human sacrifices, and required ten or more *kahunas* for the performance of its services. It was the last temple to give up its heathen worship and practice at the overthrow of idolatry in 1819.

So, when one looks at one of the best known *heiaus*, Pu-ukohola at Kawaihae, he realizes he is observing something which meant much to ancient Polynesians. Here is where an ancient people worshiped and prayed, where time itself stood still. It was one of the last temples to be erected. It happens that a former temple of the same name on the same hillsite was involved in the battles of Lonoikamekahiki over 200 years earlier, probably about 1580. The structure was rebuilt by Kamehameha, as depicted here, and is well described in the histories, particularly by Reverend William Ellis, who wrote of it in 1823. It, too, is explained that Kamehameha had not yet subdued all opposition on Hawaii, and built the temple to assure his ultimate supremacy. He had been advised to do this by Kapoukahi, Kauai's most respected prophet. Kamehameha listened and acted accordingly. In fact, the king had actually sent Haalou, the grandmother of Kaahumanu (the king's favorite wife), to Kapoukahi for his advice.

Some 200 feet below Puukohola *heiau* is the temple of Mailekini, which is a much narrower but longer edifice, 250 feet by 85 feet in size. Little is known of this much older temple. It is not even known whether or not it had any working connection with the *heiau* of Puukohola. Historians tell us that a trace of an underground passage once existed in earlier days, but the purpose of this passage is not understood. Tradition has it that Kamehameha had planned to reconstruct Mailekini, but that Prophet Kapoukahi had advised against it at the time. Consequently, all Kamehameha's efforts went into the building of Puukohola on the upper level.

Even in Waimea proper, headquarters for the Parker Ranch, there is still evidence of another ancient temple—the Uli *heiau*. Today it is little more than a low mound of stone opposite the premises of a church.

Another interesting *heiau* is on the fringes of the Parker Ranch, that of Mookini, on the land of Puuepa, Kohala. Its extra size and massive walls give one pause on inspection, and its shape is that of an irregular parallelogram, with walls of 267 feet on its west side and 250 feet on its east side. The north end is 135 feet wide, and the south end runs 112 feet. At one time its height was over 20 feet, with a width on top of 8 feet, and 30 feet at the base. It is said that the stones used in its construction were brought from Pololu Valley about ten miles away. It is understood that it took a minimum of 15,000 natives to pass the stones along by hand from man to man over that distance.

It is written that one very old man in 1841 claimed to have been a priest of the Mookini *heiau*, and he went on record as saying that ten victims were offered up in sacrifice at the temple's dedication. Several other now-gone elderly natives of the Kohala district insisted that they had been eyewitnesses to the macabre ceremony.

The presence of these ancient *heiaus* in and around the Parker Ranch holdings lend an aura of mystery and savage grandeur to the country, and one is left with imaginings of what took place here among a fast-disappearing race. Of course, none of these things transpired in the period since John Palmer Parker's time, but they were all part of the land before he came there. Parker, a lover of history who even learned and chanted many of the *meles* of the old Polynesian historians, was enthralled by things of the past. The land which became his alone was rife with ghosts of yesteryear, and he saluted his wife's people for their culture, their religion, their beliefs. And because the *heiaus* were part of all that, he saluted them, too.

The *Haole* and Cattle

Arrivals

KAWAIHAE'S HARBOR figures importantly in Hawaii's history because of another event which took place in 1790. In that year of King Kamehameha the Great's reign, an incident transpired that has since been called the Olowalu Massacre.

A foreign vessel, the *Eleanor*, commanded by Captain Metcalf, was trading on the nearby island of Maui. One of the *Eleanor*'s small boats was stolen by natives, who murdered one of the captain's sailors who was sleeping in it. Angered, the captain wanted to teach the natives a lesson, so he inveigled a swarm of native canoes to be paddled from shore to his vessel. He waited until they were within range of his guns, then ordered a thundering broadside of grapeshot. The blast killed well over a hundred natives, and wounded many.

Leaving the dead and the dying on the water, he counted the carnage as a justifiable disciplinary measure, and set sail for Hawaii, where he intended to await the return of his son, who was in command of a smaller ship, the *Fair American*, which had previously been accompanying him.

In the interim, however—and utterly unknown to Captain

Metcalf—his son's vessel, the *Fair American*, had been captured by the natives at Kawaihae. After slaughtering all of the crew, except one, the native captors had beached the ship on an isolated stretch of shore and stripped it of all its metal and other items of value. Isaac Davis was the one crewman who had escaped being murdered.

The *Eleanor* dropped her hook off Kawaihae and one John Young went ashore to seek information on the disappearance of the *Fair American*. Kamehameha detained Young in order to keep him from taking the grisly facts back to Captain Metcalf. The skipper waited offshore a reasonable length of time, then was convinced that the natives had done in Young. It was obvious that it would be foolhardy to send more men ashore in the face of such hostility. Metcalf assumed that the *Fair American* had sailed away, so he lifted anchor and set sail for China. He left with no knowledge of the death of his son and crewmen and the plundering of the schooner.

The incident remains particularly important in Hawaiian history because of the fact that both Young and Davis were held prisoners of war by Kamehameha and later were elevated to the rank of chiefs. They accepted service with Kamehameha and rendered him great aid by training Hawaiian warriors in the use of muskets and cannons, which had been acquired through barter from visiting foreign vessels. The use of the firearms gave Kamehameha a tremendous advantage in warring against his enemies at home and on other islands and had much to do with his subjugating whole areas to his will. Ultimately, he consolidated all the Islands into one single kingdom.

Kawaihae and its beach were barren land. Even before the *haole* invasion and settlement, it had little to offer in the way of the popular conception of Polynesian beauty. The famous salt ponds were here, a series of four which first captured the interest of Captain Vancouver when he delivered his cattle gift to King Kamehameha I.

The native method of obtaining salt was crude in more ways

than one. The overflow of high tide would fill the first pond, where evaporation would begin. Then, just prior to the onset of the next high tide, the Hawaiians would work with gourd cala- bashes and laboriously bail the waters into the adjoining pond, which was on slightly higher ground. Repeating this process from pond to pond, the end result was that the last and smallest pond contained water so concentrated with heavy salt crystals that they sank to the bottom. These were raked daily and spread on clean rock surfaces to dry. Ultimately, the salt was wrapped in ti leaf bundles, then hung on *auamos* (poles for carrying bun- dles) and carried away on the shoulders of natives. This Kawai- hae salt was thence transported to many areas, particularly to far-off Waipio. Later it was used in the preserving of fresh-killed beef brought down from the hills above Waimea.

The first cattle in Hawaii were delivered at Kawaihae. Cap- tain George Vancouver sailed his vessel, H.M.S. *Discovery*, into Kawaihae Harbor in 1793, just fourteen years after Captain Cook had been killed at Kealakekua Bay in 1779. Vancouver brought a gift of seven head of cattle for delivery to King Kamehameha the Great. However, the animals had not weathered the long voyage very well. They had undergone too many days of water shortage and lack of green fodder. No breeze stirred for long periods; there was nothing but glare and hot, clinging air. Suc- cessful delivery of the cattle began to shape up as pure disaster. Vancouver was sorry, truly, for he had intended to demonstrate that he was a friendly visitor, and he had anticipated that the gift of the six cows and one bull would surely express friendship.

Shortly, a chief—referred to by Vancouver as Keeaumoku— was paddled out to the ship by some of his retainers. There was no show of hostility. The paddlers brought a gift of six hogs and a supply of vegetables. Vancouver made an exchange gift of a ram, two ewes, and a ewe lamb that had been born on the ship's passage. The chief was displeased about not receiving any fire- arms or ammunition in exchange, yet he accepted the fact that King George of England had forbidden any such trading. He

did, however, advise that King Kamehameha was presently
some thirty miles to the south at Kealakekua and urged that
Vancouver remain a few days at Kawaihae to pick up additional
supplies.

Captain Vancouver agreed to this, and he wrote in his journal for February 14, 1793: "To these [Kahowmotoo's] solicitations
I in some measure consented, by promising to stay the next day,
in the expectation of not only deriving some supplies for our-
selves, but of procuring some provender for the cattle and sheep;
which in consequence of the inferior quality of the hay obtained
in Monterey, were almost starved. To this cause I attributed the
unfortunate losses we had sustained in our passage, amounting
to three rams, two ewes, a bull and a cow. These were serious
misfortunes, and in a great measure disappointed the hopes I
had entertained, from the importation of these valuable animals
into the several islands of the Pacific Ocean. Still, however, I
flattered myself with the expectation of succeeding in Owhyhee
[Hawaii], by leaving the remaining bull, with the rest of the
cows, under the protection of Tamaahmaah [Kamehameha],
who I expected would meet me at Karakakooa [Kealakekua], to
receive, and insure as far as possible, the preservation of the
animals I had on board."

Despite the gift of the smaller livestock, the chief continued
eyeing the bull and cows aboard the *Discovery*. Upon being
informed that they were being held for Kamehameha, he immediately offered to take them ashore and hold them in safety
for the king's return to Kawaihae. Due to the weakened condition of the animals, Vancouver was tempted to release them at
once. But after more consideration, and doubtful about the
chief's loyalty toward the king, Vancouver thought better of it
and resolved to present the cattle direct and in person to
Kamehameha at Kealakekua.

During the stopover Vancouver visited the village of Kawaihae and found it to be situated in a grove of tall, waving coconut
trees just back of a sandy beach. It consisted of straggling grass

houses of two types; one of small huts which furnished miserable living quarters; the other structures used for building and repairing of canoes. Between paying his respects to Kahowmotoo's wives, inspecting the large salt pond, and distributing more gift articles, Vancouver occupied his time and returned to his vessel. The accompaniment of his corporal and six armed marines had not seemed necessary at all. The captain even brought the chief and some of his ladies back aboard the *Discovery*, where he again entertained them.

Two days later, the 16th, despite the sickness of the cattle and the offer of the high chief, Vancouver set sail for the south. Kahowmotoo, attended by his favorite wife, remained aboard for the purpose of conducting the skipper to Kaiakekua (Kailua-Kona). They were beset by sporadic calms and baffling winds and lost much time. Heavy squalls lashed them.

Through his glasses, Vancouver sighted his consort vessel, the *Chatham*, tried to overtake her, then lost her again in the night. The morning of the 18th, he overtook her and managed to rendezvous with her skipper. Much-needed information was exchanged, and the report was that Kamehameha had procured some cannons and ammunition from certain traders and had now emplaced them back of stone walls at Kealakekua. It was said that the battlements were set up in the same place where the habitations of the native priests had been destroyed by foreigners shortly after the killing of Captain Cook. This made it sound all the more ominous—and Vancouver took the news as an ill omen.

More calms, then light, baffling winds continued to detain the *Discovery*. Oppressive heat sickened the animals even further. Vancouver had reason to fear that the delivery of his cattle to King Kamehameha would never become a reality. Finally an incident occurred that got at least a portion of the ailing cattle ashore. No better form of documentation of this episode is available than that in the captain's journal, dated February 18, 1793, where he explained in detail:

"A circumstance now occurred that contributed to make me infinitely more dissatisfied with this irksome detention from the shore. The only bull that remained, and a cow that had brought forth a dead calf, were no longer able to stand on their legs, and it was evident that if a speedy opportunity did not offer itself for relieving them by sending them on shore, their lives could not possibly be preserved. The loss, particularly of the bull, would have been a cruel disappointment to my wishes; but as favorable circumstances often take place when we least expected, so it was on this occasion.

"In the afternoon of the 19th we were visited by many canoes, though at the distance of 8 or 9 leagues from the land. In one of these was a chief named Kalaimamahu, half brother to Tamaahmaah [Kamehameha], and chief of the district of Hilo. To him and to his friends I made such presents as were considered by Kahowmotoo highly suitable to his rank, and which were accepted with marks of great approbation and content. This induced me to hope that, by his good offices, I should be enabled to get these poor animals conveyed to the shore. As his canoe was sufficiently large and roomy, I requested he would consent to their being put into it, but to my great surprise a thousand evasions and excuses were immediately started. Anxious for the future advantages these people would derive by the propagation of these animals, I probably discovered much earnestness, whilst endeavoring to prevail with Crymamahoo to lend me his assistance, in securing to himself and countrymen so important a benefit.

"This he certainly perceived, but possessing no desire to oblige, nor any patriotic zeal, he was only studious to turn my entreaties to his own particular advantage. After Kahowmotoo had anxiously interfered, but with the same success, I offered Crymamahoo (well knowing that avarice is a predominant passion with many of these islanders) a moderate recompense only, for allowing his canoe to perform this service. He instantly waived all his former objections, and the bull and cow were soon comfortably placed in his canoe, in which there were some vegetables that the bull ate, seemingly with much appetite; this gave me great pleasure, as I was now in hopes that he would soon recover by the help of proper nourishing food, which the shore abundantly supplied."

The next morning, February 20, 1793, Vancouver set sail southward for the purpose of finding King Kamehameha and delivering the remaining five cows to him. On the 21st, when the *Discovery* was off Tyahtatooa (Kailua-Kona), Vancouver was intercepted by the monarch himself. He noted it in his diary:

"About noon I was honored with the presence of Tamaahmaah, the king of Owhyhee [Hawaii], whose approach had been announced some time before his arrival. Not only from Captain King's description, but also from my own memory, as far as it would serve me, I expected to have recognized my former acquaintance by the most savage countenance we had hitherto seen amongst these people; but I was agreeably surprised in finding that his riper years had softened that stern ferocity which his younger days had exhibited, and had changed his general deportment to an address characteristic of an open, cheerful and sensible mind; combined with great generosity, and goodness of disposition. An alteration not unlike that I have before had occasion to notice in the character of Pomurrey at Otaheite.

"Tamaahmaah came on board in a very large canoe, accompanied by John Young, an English seaman, who appeared to be not only a great favourite, but to possess no small degree of influence with this great chief. Terrehooa, who had been sent to deliver the bull and cow to the king, was also of the party, and informed me that the cow had died in her passage to the island, but that the bull arrived safe, and was lodged in a house where he ate and drank heartily."

Vancouver presented King Kamehameha and his chiefs with many gifts, but made it a point to see that none of them remained aboard for the night. He well knew the fate of other foreign skippers who had made this mistake. At dark the Islanders returned to shore in high spirits, and the *Discovery*'s captain sailed his vessel on farther south. By morning, the 22nd, they were abreast of Kealakekua and were visited by a veritable armada of canoes loaded with natives. Vancouver came about and dropped anchor.

This being the residence of King Kamehameha, it was not surprising that the monarch himself was in the lead canoe rowed by eighteen paddles on each side. Under Kamehameha's direction, the war canoes paraded en masse around the waiting Vancouver. It was a solemn and dignified procession, with Captain Vancouver wondering what it was all about. When ten canoes drew up in a line under the *Discovery*'s stern, Kamehameha came aboard and extended his hand to the ship's captain. There was much reassuring of one another's good faith and intent. Kamehameha presented Vancouver with four very handsome feathered helmets and ordered ten of the large canoes to discharge their cargoes of hogs to the deck of the ship. This involved ninety hogs in all, a supply of fresh meat much needed by the visitors.

Vancouver relates in his journal how he then reciprocated with more gifts of his own. He wrote:

"The remaining livestock I had on board, consisting of five cows, two ewes and a ram, were sent on shore in some of his canoes; these were all in a healthy state though in low condition, and as I flattered myself the bull would recover, I had little doubt of their succeeding to the utmost of my wishes. I cannot avoid mentioning the pleasure I received, in the particular attention paid by Tammahmaah to the placing of these animals in the canoes. This business was principally done by himself; after which he gave the strictest injunctions to his people who had charge of them, to pay implicit obedience to the directions of our butcher, who was sent to attend their landing. At the departure of these canoes, I was unacquainted with the extent of Tamaahmaah's intended compliment. In addition to his magnificent present of provisions, other canoes were now ordered alongside, from which a large quantity of cloth, mats, and other articles of their own manufacture, were delivered into the ship; but we were so much incommoded, that there was no possibility of taking care of these valuables, and on promising to receive them on a future day, the king permitted them to be returned to the shore, giving particular charge to one of his attendants, to whom they were intrusted, to be very careful of them, as they belonged to me, and not to himself."

These heretofore unseen and unknown horned animals were brought up onto the beach, and the natives surrounded them in wide-eyed wonder. Immediately after the cattle got their first feel of terra firma, they braced their legs, sniffed at the ground, then swung their heads in ecstasy. Instantly, despite their weakened condition, they began cavorting and milling as though beset by demons. The natives took this for ferociousness and scattered for safety. Some sought refuge in the nearby coconut trees; others plunged into the surf. The cattle went on gamboling on shore, and the natives didn't readily interpret the scene as one of animals simply long-sick for the feel of solid earth under their hooves.

Kamehameha was to come aboard the *Discovery* again the following morning, but failed to show up. Instead, he sent a messenger aboard with word that two of the *wahines* (females) who had remained overnight with the sailors had stolen several articles from the vessel. He pointed out that he already had one of the girls in custody and would see to it that the stolen items would be safely returned. Captain Vancouver was also advised that another loss had been sustained in the cattle shipment.

Apropos of the return of the stolen goods and the cattle loss, Vancouver wrote in his journal that February:

"This was done about breakfast time, after which he [Kamehameha] spent the remainder of the day with me, and gave me the unwelcome intelligence that the bull for whose recovery I was so very solicitous, was dead. On this mortifying occasion I much regretted that I had not followed the advice of Kahowmoto, from whose connection with the king I most probably might have relied with perfect security on his offers of taking charge of the cattle at Toeaigh. Two of the young cows, however, appeared to be in calf; this encouraged me to hope that his loss would be repaired by one of them bringing forth a male. The finest of the two ewes, I was now informed was killed by a dog the day after the cattle were landed, whose life was instantly forfeited for the transgression."

Despite the losses and the sorry condition of the animals, Kamehameha received them with pleasure and *mahalos* (thanks). The saga of the cattle had begun, and it was to change the whole character of the Big Isle.

History doesn't record whether or not one of the original five cows dropped a male calf, but it does show that Captain Vancouver made sure of the cattle venture's success by returning again to Hawaii the following year and bringing additional cattle. His journal entry of January 15, 1794 reads:

"After the large canoes had delivered their acceptable cargoes, they received and took to the shore [Kealakekua] the live cattle, which I had been more successful in bringing from New Albion than on the former occasion. These consisted of a young bull nearly full grown, two fine cows, and two very fine bull calves, all in high condition; as likewise five rams, and five ewe sheep. Two of each of these, with most of the black cattle, were given to the king; and as those I had brought last year had thrived exceedingly well; the sheep having bred, and one of the cows having brought forth a cow calf; I had little doubt, by this second importation, of having at length effected the very desirable object of establishing in this island a breed of those valuable animals."

In any event, Kamehameha had, from the start, agreed with Vancouver that the bovines should be protected until they had greatly multiplied. The king declared a *kapu* (taboo) upon all of them. Death would be the penalty for anyone either injuring or killing one of the animals. This decree was the protection which led to the thousands of maverick cattle that ultimately roamed the plains, valleys, and forests of northern Hawaii. It was from these wild beasts, in later years, that John Palmer Parker selected, captured, and improved a new breed which finally made up the vast herds that swarm over today's Parker Ranch.

One last bit of evidence on Vancouver's protection arrangement with King Kamehameha is found in the captain's journal, dated February 23, 1794. It follows:

"Anxious lest the object I had so long had in view should hereafter be defeated; namely, that of establishing a breed of sheep, cattle, and other European animals in these islands, which with so much difficulty, trouble, and concern, I had at length succeeded so far as to import in good health and in a thriving condition; I demanded, that they should be tabooed for ten years, with a discretionary power in the king alone to appropriate a certain number of the males of each species, in case that sex became predominant, to the use of his own table; but that in so doing the women should not be precluded partaking of them, as the intention of their being brought to the island was for the general use and benefit of every inhabitant of both sexes, as soon as their numbers should be sufficiently increased to allow of a general distribution amongst the people. This was unanimously approved of, and faithfully promised to be observed with one exception only; that with respect to the meat of these several animals, the women were to be put on the same footing as with their dogs and fowls; they were to be allowed to eat of them, but not of the identical animal that men had partaken, or of which they were to partake."

4

John Palmer Parker

O N M A Y 1, 1 7 9 0, in Newton, Massachusetts, not
far up the Charles River from Boston, a son was born
to Samuel and Ann Palmer Parker. They named the
child John Palmer Parker. The parents were descendants of New England founding fathers who had first come to the
North American shores around 1630. Sailing was in the infant's
blood, for the father had inherited whaling ships from his fore-
bears, and the mother was descended from shipyard owners and
operators in Southampton, England. It was the post-Revolution-
ary era—the Federalist Period—an exciting time in which to be
alive.

The child had a solid start in life, for his parents were well
educated, maintained a spacious, well-ordered home, and were
eager seekers of knowledge in many fields divorced from their
own private interests. The prime legacy they left young John
was an ever seeking mind and a yen for travel. He early became
an omnivorous reader and wide rover. Because his father was so
involved with the whaling business and away at that seaport
much of the time, young John ultimately grew extremely close
to his mother, a woman of understanding and sympathy.

Young John had a shy, tilted smile. He was rather quiet, and
his voice was soft and flat, but there was something in it that
made people listen. With maturity, he overcame his shyness, but

his humility remained. Too, his voice took on a resonant depth that gave it authority. The boy was graced with the gift of making friends. The hired hands on the old homestead were soon teaching him how to break ground for planting, how to harvest crops, how to milk a cow, and do many of the chores on a small piece of farmland.

As a teen-age lad he was long-legged, raw-boned, and champing at the bit to go places and do things of significance. He loved Boston's harbor and all the tall ships riding at berth there. The sea beckoned—the clean rasp of salt air, and the cry of the horn of each arriving or departing vessel.

He early became a dedicated collector of artifacts in connection with the early history of the land in which he had been born. Anything to do with the Indians and items touching on the Revolutionary War caught his special attention. As a youngster, he avidly amassed an assortment of Indian weapons and military artifacts.

He spent his first early years at Framingham Academy in eastern Massachusetts where, and when the opportunity afforded itself on Sundays, he went down to the docks and wharves of Boston harbor, combing them for interesting sights, savoring their sounds and smells. The sight of the high-masted sailing ships sent his blood coursing.

As a student, young John excelled at mathematics and history. Upon leaving Framingham in 1808, at the age of eighteen, John was employed by his father in the family business. He kept the books for the firm, but his deep-down wish was to join the whaling fleet at the first opportunity.

Young John finally wangled one short whaling excursion into coastal waters. The trip proved distasteful in more ways than one. There proved to be hardly any whales, the stench of boiling blubber was repugnant, and the junket was utterly devoid of romance, color, or real interest.

But John still had his eyes riveted on the spars and sails of those proud merchant ships which would be visiting distant seas, far continents, exotic islands. He made his move, signing aboard a New England vessel destined for Pacific Ocean ports. His job was that of captain's clerk. The ship was ticketed for a first stop in the Northwest where it would take on a cargo of furs, then would sail to the Sandwich Islands to pick up a load of sandalwood.

Once at sea, John Parker's work aboard ship involved a lot more than merely clerking for the captain and keeping the vessel's log. His duties ran the gamut—working with the crew in wind-blown rigging, in the dank hold, on wave-lashed decks, and he learned every facet of keeping a sailing ship in operation.

After months of sailing—having rounded the Horn and nosing northward into calmer waters—the ship took on its cargo of furs in the Pacific Northwest. It then headed for the Sandwich Isles far to the southwest. After more weeks of sailing on bright, trackless seas, they finally arrived off the west coast of Hawaii in 1809.

In the distance, John Parker could see the lush green islands which Captain Cook had named in honor of his financial backer, the Earl of Sandwich. The lush, tropical look of the shores and the blue of the water were all John had anticipated—and more. He became thoroughly enchanted with the region and with the people.

The early 1800s were the heyday of sandalwood trading between King Kamehameha I and sea captains from all over the world. The fragrant wood was at a tremendous premium, particularly in the Orient for furniture making and incense burning. Everything was basically on a barter basis, for the Hawaiians had no monetary means of exchange. The sandalwood cargoes were traded for porcelain, tea, silks, and many other items.

The trading ship rounded into waters of Kawaihae. In the morning Parker went ashore with a party. He always had an eye alert for golden opportunities, and now he was observing armies of Polynesian natives dragging logs of sandalwood down the lonely, windswept roads from the uplands above Waimea. Many were carrying branches and limbs of the sandalwood trees on their backs. These natives were commoners, doing the bidding of their chiefs—and all for no pay.

Dragging and packing the heavy loads down the hillsides was backbreaking work. John Parker studied them closely, sympathized, and wondered what they would use for barter once the sandalwood forests were wholly depleted. And the region would be deforested, for King Kamehameha I had commanded his chiefs to make the people cut and cut as if there would be no tomorrow. The approaching depletion was already obvious, for no full cargo was available for the vessel at this time. Disappointed, the skipper weighed anchor and left for other waters.

But the ship left without John Parker, who was so totally infatuated with what he'd seen of Hawaii that he jumped ship with all his belongings. Parker knew that foreigners were not welcome as permanent residents on the island, but he took the calculated risk anyhow. He secreted himself in the nearby forest until long after the vessel had slipped below the horizon, then he put himself at the mercy of the natives and the land.

John soon won the friendship and confidence of those he met. They accepted him, and he accepted them. He liked the soft weather, the lush green of the thicketed area, the flowers rioting in wild profusion, and even the brooding mountains in the distance. He told of these thing in later years, and his estimate of the Islands never diminished.

In short order the natives helped John build a small *hale* (house) to live in temporarily. He tilled an area around the hut and planted seeds which took root. He concentrated on gaining a working knowledge of the Polynesian language. He made the friendship of a native who had entree to King Kamehameha's court, and soon the king himself was made aware of the *malihini's* (newcomer's) presence on the island. In time, the monarch sent for the *haole*.

John went with misgivings, for the king was notoriously

suspicious of foreigners—and had a right to be. Too many times in the past his land had been visited by an element of men that represented a vicious and nefarious world. His trusting people and his kingdom in general had been vulnerable to arrogant, criminal *baoles,* and he had naturally developed a jaundiced attitude toward them.

Despite this, John's visit at court was a success. Word of his character and capacity for work had preceded him, and he was well received by the monarch. Kamehameha saw much to admire in this stranger. Parker was massive—not so much in size as in impact. He was intense but in control.

John saw much in the king, too, for here was an aging man —still hale and strong—and still the forthright leader of his people; he was a man who had united an island nation that had been torn by strife and misunderstanding for many generations.

John was offered the job of managing the royal fish ponds at Honaunau, adjacent to the City of Refuge, just south of Kealakekua Bay. His responsibility was to see that the ponds were kept clean and abundantly stocked with fish. He accepted the offer and worked at it with vigor and dedication. Unremitting toil was his forte, as always. Meanwhile, he kept an eye alert for better, bigger opportunities.

In addition to working prodigiously at the chores delegated to him, John also strove to cement his friendship with the commoners as well as with the *alii* at the royal court. With all the Hawaiians he met and dealt with, he was, in their tongue, *kanakanui*—a big man physically, and with leadership ability to match.

But that old feeling of restlessness began stirring again, that desire to see what lay on the other side of the horizon. It was 1811, just past John Parker's twenty-first birthday, and he was ripening for a change—maybe only a temporary one—but still a sight of something else. A merchant ship of the Winship and Davis Company sailed into the Hawaiian harbor, and he went aboard to see people of his own kind from New England.

John talked to members of the crew whom he knew, and again he got caught up in the nostalgia for sailing. Possibly the feel of a moving deck under his feet made his roving spirit catch fire again. He signed on for a voyage to the Orient.

As the vessel sailed away from the Big Island's shore, John was still enamored of Hawaii, and he intended to return. But the blood in his veins throbbed for more adventure at sea and in far ports. Possibly he thought he could get this fever out of his system once and for all.

But John's luck deserted him after the ship dropped anchor in Canton Harbor. The War of 1812 was at its height, and the British raised a blockade to all shipping traffic. For almost two years John's ship was compelled to remain harbor-bound. It stands to reason that, with John's ambitious temperament, he chaffed throughout all this inaction. But, finally, just before the close of the war in January, 1815, the vessel was allowed to clear the harbor and sail away.

The Winship and Davis merchant ship voyaged again for the Sandwich Islands and made port at Kawaihae just before New Year's Day of 1815. John Parker was back from the long sailing, unscathed, but as old as twenty-five could be. He knew by then that simply sailing the seas was a life without meaning. He needed and wanted something solid and secure—something to put roots into. He went ashore and was once more on the island which had become so dear to him.

Dreams for success and prosperity began to build within John anew. He had to think of the future, of the years ahead. But he knew he still had one major problem to surmount before he could have any sense of security. One had to have the approval of the king if one were to survive here at all. It was the law of the land. If a man were not under the "protection" of the monarch, he stood in danger of being ordered from the Islands on instant notice. For that matter, he ran the risk of a lot of other dire penalties, too—including death or imprisonment.

It must be remembered that when Parker first visited these

Islands, little had changed from prediscovery days. The natives lived in much the same way that their ancestors had lived. Few *haoles* were in the Islands at all, and even the first American missionaries had not yet arrived. Parker had to again seek among the Hawaiians for some means of subsisting and making a living.

From his previous visit, he had a working knowledge of the native tongue, but it would avail him little without King Kamehameha's approval of his return. The mark of the king was everywhere. All John had to do was to look shoreward and see the temple Puukohola which the monarch had built in honor of the war god, Kukailimoku. The people were still totally subservient to the king, so it was imperative that John obtain the sovereign's approval.

A trip to Kailua, on the Kona coast where Kamehameha still held court, was of utmost importance. John resolved to go and state his business. Fortunately, John had the talent for being aggressive without being offensive. To arrange for a meeting at court, he availed himself of the friendship of Peter Davis, who was also a premissionary pioneer of the Islands. Peter Davis was the son of Isaac Davis, the only survivor of a sailing ship, the *Fair American*, which had been sunk by the natives in years gone by. Peter had made a niche for himself in the Hawaiian scheme of things, and, as a friendly *haole*, had the favor of Kamehameha. As a sort of liaison officer, Peter Davis attempted to pave the way for John Parker.

John rented a horse from Peter Davis and rode the dirt trail to Kailua to see the king. He nourished the hope that, like several other *haoles* before him, he just might fit in with the monarch's plans for development of this little isolated nation.

Upon arrival at the court, Kamehameha's guards met him, asked what he wanted, and took the message to the monarch. Again John's personality, appearance, and command of the Hawaiian language stood him in good stead, for he was quickly allowed to come into the royal presence.

John was more than a little surprised to see the *alii* wearing such fine un-Polynesian raiment; more so than during his first visit to these Sandwich Islands. Most of them wore garments made of foreign—European, Asian, or American—fabrics. It was obvious that even more importing was being done from other lands. Whereas the commoners were wearing little other than tapa cloth (fabric made from the inner bark of a kind of mulberry tree), here was a dearth of tapa in any form. He noted, too, for the second time, the beauty of these *alii* personages; they had royalty stamped all over them. The women were beautifully formed and adorned, and more than one caught his eye. John recognized that his two-year hiatus from Hawaii while in Canton had certainly brought on some changes in the habits of these people. Trade and barter had picked up, and John could easily see that becoming a part of this structure would be a sensible and profitable move.

During the dialogue between John and the king, Kamehameha apparently reassured himself that the big *haole* was friendly, quiet, wise, and honest. He also obviously appreciated the foreigner's integrity, and nodded his promise to befriend him. This second court meeting between the two of them seemed reassuring. Yet there appeared to be doubt in the monarch's mind with reference to the newcomer's intention to remain permanently on the Island. Maybe the *haole* would suddenly change his mind and unexpectedly sail away again.

For a few seconds John thought that he would be refused. In later years, Parker often reminisced about this fateful moment. In any event, he quickly explained to the king and the advisers at his side, "There's a difference between a man on the go and a man on the run. My running days aboard ship are back of me." He told it this way to the monarch—and the decision was final.

He and Parker were communicating better now. Among the other things which Kamehameha was interested in was the fact that the foreigner had brought an American musket and ammunition ashore and would be able to shoot the wild cattle which so thickly roamed the canyons and slopes of this land. The Kohala forests around Waiapuka abounded with wild cattle, and that was where John was currently staying. Beef was there for the taking, and it could be a boon to the bartering for other goods. Tallow and hides, too, were at a premium.

The result was that John Parker was commissioned to help with the supplying of garden vegetables, taro, meats, and hides for both local and foreign consumption. He was the first man allowed by the king to shoot cattle. So, in 1815 John Parker was at the floodtide of his youth with a new and promising job on a strange island far out on the Pacific. He loved the land, he loved the people—and his ambition knew no bounds.

For these considerations Kamehameha offered John a parcel of land and a grass *hale* to live in Niulii, Kohala, adjacent to Pololu Valley. This was some measure of the king's high regard for John, for Niulii was close to that region so dear to the monarch's heart—the area where he had spent his childhood after being smuggled there to escape King Alapainui's assassins. The specific parcel of land involved was called Waiapuka, signifying "spring water"—and it presently became John's home.

John Parker was particularly interested in the fine spring water which was available at Waiapuka, and envisioned what it could do for taro planting and vegetables. The contract was made between the king and the foreigner, with the blessings of the king's chief *kahunas*.

By digging irrigation ditches and lining them with stone and mud clay, John Parker soon was able to water the highly tillable soil. Not long after his planting, he had lush crops of both taro and garden vegetables. His judgment of the worth of the spring water proved eminently correct, and now he was in business.

The earliest archives point out that Parker "fished and cultivated the soil and supplied sundry ships with food." It is understood by most authorities that "cultivating the soil" meant truck gardening, no easy thing without the aid of farm animals for plowing, harvesting, and marketing. After all, only a few

years had elapsed since Captain Richard Cleveland had landed
the first horses on the Island, and they had been permitted to
run wild into the dense forests and on the wide plains, as had
happened to the first cattle which Captain George Vancouver
had put ashore sixteen years previously. The animals appeared
to represent no value to the Hawaiian people—not even as
beasts of burden. So, with some native help, John Parker by
unremitting hand labor sweated out the truck gardening the
hard, laborious way.

"Land isn't worth anything," Parker insisted, "unless you do
something with it." Then he proceeded to till it. Life had taken
on a new meaning, and his roving days were certainly past.

As time went by, John—like many other unmarried, sensitive men—began to yearn for a woman helpmate; he wanted a
woman to love, cherish, and share his life with. She could give
him sons and daughters as heirs, something to build for. So he
began his search for a desirable woman.

His search ended up in his wooing and winning the hand of
the Chieftess Keliikipikaneokaolohaka—shortened later to
"Kipikane"—granddaughter of Kamehameha I and Kaneikapolei. Her father was Chief Kahaaulani, and her mother was
Kahiwa Kaneikapolei. It was a fast courtship with Kipikane's
parents gratified over the prospects of the marriage. She was a
small young woman beside his raw-boned figure. She had a
pleasing personality, and she loved John devotedly.

They were wed in a traditional Hawaiian ceremony wherein
the final nuptials are pronounced when the *kahuna* places a
white tapa cloak over the shoulders of the wedded couple. It was
in 1816 on a sun-washed summer afternoon that the marriage of
two sincere people from totally different backgrounds, culture,
and race was to start a dynasty new to Hawaii.

At first the newlyweds lived with Kipikane's father and
mother in that area—a traditional Polynesian custom in those
days. John sought his own home again a little later, for his deep
sense of independence was undiminished.

King Kamehameha I was thoroughly pleased over the marriage and welcomed both John and Kipikane on their occasional court visits. Later, when the missionaries arrived in 1820, Parker arranged for a Christian marriage. He loved Kipikane deeply and wanted more than the pagan ceremony to seal their togetherness. Kipikane was happy over the decision, and they were married a second time. In this additional ceremony, incidentally, she took the Christian name of Rachel and was thereafter spoken of as Rachel Kipikane.

The first child born to John and Kipikane was a daughter. They named the baby Mary Ann Kaulalani Parker. This was in the year 1819, the same year that saw the death of the *alii* who had so befriended Parker—King Kamehameha the Great.

That year was also significant to John Parker, for it was the year when he was one of the only two *haoles* present at that momentous feast at Kailua, the capital, when Liholiho (King Kamehameha II) broke the age-old eating taboo and so abolished the ancient Polynesian religion. Prior to this, the strict taboo had prohibited men and women from eating together. This had been a dramatic event, for Liholiho had sat down and eaten openly with the chiefs and chieftesses. John was seeing history being made. And, unknown to himself, he was beginning to make history on his own account—Hawaiian history.

Mary Ann was cherished and adored. However, eight years were to elapse without another birth, and Kipikane felt badly about not presenting her man with a male heir. Traditionally, her own race counted a man-child as all-important. John, too, wished for more children, and were it not that he was so understanding and sympathetic, Kipikane's plight would have been more sorry during those interminable eight years of childlessness. She had begun to think that her having married out of her ancestral lines was bringing on this punishment from her gods.

.The times were colorful and exciting in the Kohala country. For the young, sensitive, and high-keyed Mary Ann Parker, her days of girlhood were a joy. She was still a very young girl when she rode with the *paniolos* (cowboys) around the paddocks and on the range. She adored the imported *espagnols* who were working the herds and teaching the local Hawaiian cowboys how to properly handle cattle and horses. She was captivated by their politeness and courtesy, and she delighted in the sight of their costumes of broad-brimmed sombreros, bright silk sashes, spur-jangling boots, and multicolored ponchos. It all met with the senior Parkers' approval, for the *paniolos* were cautiously protective of Mary Ann at all times and reveled in her attentions. By nature, she was a lovable *hapa*-Hawaiian girl (*hapa* meaning "half"), taking after her mother more than her father. Oddly, she had a reputation for shying away from *haoles*, and mixing mostly with people of her mother's race; and these were mainly of the Hawaiian chief families.

In any event, her very existence had now given John Parker's life an additional meaning; he had an heir.

5

Parker and the *Paniolos*

B Y 1 8 3 0 the shortsighted orders of Island chiefs had reduced sandalwood trade to almost nothing; a quarter of a century of harvesting every sandalwood tree and sapling had denuded the region of the long-time bonanza. The monarchy had changed again; the young Prince Kauikeaouli, son of Kamehameha I and his sacred wife, had been proclaimed king on June 6, 1825. Kaahumanu continued in the regency during the king's minority. Both she and the new young king—now Kamehameha III—saw the foolhardiness of the sandalwood harvesting, and put a taboo on the cutting of it. Prior to this the natives had been forced to neglect their cultivating of taro crops, and their fishing had ceased, and now there was a serious shortage of food on the land. The death penalty was put upon any more gathering of sandalwood by commoners.

The *alii* of Hawaii had gotten themselves into desperate economic problems. They had plunged deeply into debt by buying recklessly on credit. They owed heavily for items like furniture, carpets, household fixtures, silk, wool, cotton goods, jewelry, guns, ammunition, and a multitude of other imported things. These were goods which they had felt they could not do without.

With this acute economic dilemma facing them, the native

rulers put an even greater value and importance on their newly found bartering expedient—beef. There was a promise of solving the debt problem. The wild animals, as well as Parker's semidomesticated ones, were suddenly at an incredible premium.

Kamehameha's *kapu* on the ranging beasts was strict, for the monarch was in a position to deal out the heaviest of punishment for law infractions. Within ten years the increase in numbers of wild cattle was astonishing. Both the lush growth of natural feed and the friendly climate were vital factors.

By 1813, twenty years after being introduced, the animals had so multiplied that they had become a nuisance, devouring and trampling the natives' crops of potatoes, ravishing their taro patches, and in short, raising havoc with whatever was planted. The Sandwich Islanders were compelled to drive the cattle back from the inhabited areas, and when that didn't work they built stone fences in some places to ward them off. In regions where koa trees flourished, the branches were cut, then twisted and crisscrossed into rude fences for holding off the invading animal hordes. To this day some of the remnants of such fences are still visible in Waimea and its environs.

Not only had the cattle become destructive to crops, but they had also become so wild that they were a menace to the lives of the natives themselves. By 1815 people stayed out of certain regions where the wild bulls were prone to attack. The herds were now scattered over the plains between Mauna Kea and Mauna Loa, to say nothing of the slopes of the Kohala Mountains. Hualalai had its share of the roving beasts. But particularly dangerous were the bovines in the deep mountain forest areas. A man took his life in his hands when he invaded these thicketed regions where sharp-horned cattle reigned supreme over all they surveyed.

One of the solid markets for salt beef was found in supplying the whaling fleets which had started their fifty-year stretch of Island calls. They wintered in the Islands and replenished their stores of water, wood, fresh produce, and beef. Hawaii began to thrive on the ships' wants, yet indebtedness continued to mount at the royal court.

As inventive and imaginative as Parker was, his early production of beef could not keep up with the great and fast-increasing demand. He was a genius in his own right, but he needed help. He had dire need of skilled horsemen and cowboys to assist in the work. The more he hunted and killed, plus the more he developed and enlarged his herd, the greater grew the demand for beef. There seemed no end to the market. The need for assistance grew accordingly.

Help finally came from the most unexpected of sources. Massive indebtedness at the royal court made it mandatory that something be done to increase revenue. More beef—which also meant more tallow and hides—seemed assuredly one of the better answers, so Kamehameha III sought to help with the employment problem on the ranges. He sent to California for Mexican, Indian, and Spanish vaqueros to come over to the Islands to teach the Hawaiian men how to handle horses and cattle— anything to improve the cattle business.

When the colorful vaqueros arrived, the Hawaiian learners were quick to emulate the costumes of these strange *haoles*; everything from the brilliant woolen ponchos to the slashed leggings, brightly colored sashes, bandanas over their heads, and floppy hats with broad brims. In that they were being taught and instructed by, as they called them, the *Espanols*, they began calling themselves *paniolos*—a perversion of the former word. They were a colorful element of people in an exciting era.

With all the king's horses and cattle running wild over the mesas and in the forests and canyons, there was much stock for these *paniolos* to work with. Their first major chore was to capture the king's wild horses, then to break them to saddle. This was no easy task, for the animals were direct descendants of the tough mustangs, or broncos, of the mainland's Southwest. The beasts had known no masters and were stalwart fighters against being brought to halter. Their reputation was such that the natives called them *li'o*—a Hawaiian word meaning wide eyed or wild eyed. In fact, *lio* ultimately became the native name for horse.

The *Espanols* soon taught the Hawaiians all the arts of the cowboy: how to tan leather with the bark of koa and ohia trees; how to braid rawhide quirts and lariats; how to build saddles along the lines of the Mexican type. The Mexican-Spanish influence prevailed even to the extent that the Hawaiians modeled their wagons after the stick-framed Mexican carts. For wheels, they hewed cross sections of koa trees, rounded them more evenly, and put axles through their centers.

The spine-crushing days of packing beef on the back or shoulder waned when the *paniolos* learned to rope and tame steers to haul the wagons. Beef, tallow, and hides were then more easily and rapidly transported down from the high Waimea regions to the waiting ships at Kawaihae. At that point, that other *haole* in the employ of Kamehameha, John Young, took over and saw to the distribution to the king's vessels, merchant ships, and whalers.

So, during this new era, the sagacious John Parker devoted much of his time to going into the forests and valleys and shooting the king's wild cattle. The long royal *kapu* on longhorns of the Spanish type had led to their wandering off into the vast, uninhabited wild regions, where they had become mavericks in every sense of the word. The stock had inbred and soon developed into broken herds of long-legged, slabsided cattle. Fully matured steers would hardly average over 500 pounds dressed weight—but while on the hoof, they were a threat and a hazard.

This danger didn't prevent Parker from trekking up into the rugged forest regions to get beef. Hawaiians, too, were now eating red meat despite the fact that they had, for generations, been confining their eating to fish, pig, and poi. The local consumption of beef, however, didn't begin to compare with the market found aboard the incoming vessels. Ships' crews, often poorly fed at sea, rejoiced at the sight of fresh beef. But, more importantly, the ships' masters began accepting larger and larger quantities of salted beef. All this, of course, was in exchange for goods brought in from foreign ports.

The taking of beef was hard, dangerous work, for the animals were vicious and wild and would often turn upon an attacker. They were lean and rugged, capable of concealing themselves from sight in the almost impenetrable tangles and trees of deep canyons.

But the sturdy, indomitable John Parker would not be daunted. Each time he shot a bull or cow, he cut away the meat from the carcass and hauled it to where he could salt it and pack it in barrels. Salt was no great problem those days, and the sizable pond at Kawaihae served Parker well.

As he began to enlist more help in his inland excursions, his production of beef stepped up accordingly. It was not long before the former sandalwood bearers were changed into beef bearers, and the waiting ships were quick to accept the substitute.

In the role of King Kamehameha's *konohiki* (agent), Parker continued to kill beef and salt down more and more of it for local consumption as well as for supplying the vessels. With his usual foresight and business acumen, the *konohiki* took his "salary" in the form of selected live cattle. These he fenced in, and the animals he couldn't tame he shot for their hides, tallow, and meat. He was very choosy in his selection of the animals, kept an eye out for the very best for breeding, and soon began domesticating many of them.

In the early years the cattle were the joint property of the king and the Hawaiian government. The right to slaughter was leased or sold to private parties. Hunters were paid from $1.00 to $1.25 for each bull hide and $1.00 for each cow hide. These prices covered hides correctly dried and hauled to a central point, where they were collected for further shipment.

Of course, in years to come, the slaughtering and shipping

of cattle stepped up tremendously. A quick survey of the ascendancy of this business is found in old archives: during the first six months of 1859, 22,170 pounds of hide at 25 cents a pound were exported. The following figures give an estimate of the size of the herds in this era: 8,000 tame cattle; 12,000 wild; 1,200 horses; 3,000 sheep.

Parker was fortunate in these times in having an outstanding man working with him in the cattle-killing business. Jack Purdy had come to Hawaii aboard a whaling vessel, and had, like Parker himself, jumped ship at Kawaihae. They were a highly effective team in the dangerous business of slaughtering the wild animals on the ranges and in the valleys, and bringing them down to the Waimea area. In reality they were the first true cowboys of Hawaii. Purdy himself was so adept at the work that it is reported that he outslew Parker by quite a margin and made more pay at it. Purdy's chief strategy was to set traps over lava pits, or sometimes catch the animals in swamps where deep mud would then mire them. He married a Hawaiian woman by the name of Koka, and, some great cowmen developed from the ensuing family.

Mary Low, the great-granddaughter of John and Kipikane Parker, describes him:

"Back in Waimea, Jack Purdy told them a story as he drank draught after draught of small glasses of gin—which seemed to have no effect upon him other than to draw him out from his usual taciturnity. The story is a long one, but the substance of it is this. An Englishman named Brenchley heard of Jack's prowess. He was a man of fortune, a great traveler of herculean strength, an indefatigable explorer, who had been in Hawaii some time. He took Jack for a guide and proved that he could do anything or go anywhere that the guide could. One day Jack proposed that they go out, taking only their guns and blankets.

"They went towards Mauna Loa and subsisted on geese, ducks and plover. At length their powder was exhausted, and Brenchley asked how they were to get something to eat. Jack took him for a twenty-mile walk to a swampy piece of ground into which Brenchley sank to his knees. He was told to remain there while the guide went into the thick brush from which there soon came a wild bull with an eye of fire and a tail erect. The animal plunged into the swamp and stuck fast, and Jack said, 'There is our dinner!'

"The traveler did not see how he was to get his beef, but the guide gathered some brush and, twisting it into two bundles, put one on the mud and stepped on it. Then he cast the other bundle ahead and stepped on that, picking up the first bundle and casting it before him. In this way he reached the bull and, drawing his knife, cut the animal's throat and soon sliced off some pieces of beef. Returning to firm ground in the same manner as he had gone to the bull, he kindled a fire and in a short time invited Brenchley to dinner. The traveler, having found a man who could beat him in daring, started next morning for Hilo on his way to Honolulu."

Oddly, Jack Purdy might well have wound up with a massive cattle ranch of his own. He had much the same opportunity as John Parker, for his wife, too, was of royal Hawaiian blood— half-Hawaiian, that is—and she owned much land. Purdy was a top cattle hunter, but he had a weakness for the bottle that he allowed to defeat him. He once traded an acre of land for a gallon of wine. Eventually he sold his land to the teetotaler, John Parker, who was already dreaming of a cattle dynasty.

But drink or no drink, Jack Purdy was a powerhouse of a man, and no other two men could team up so successfully at cattle hunting as Parker and himself. Both of them knew the Kohala Mountain and Mauna Kea regions thoroughly. Purdy didn't have Parker's dream of a cattle dynasty, but the whaler-turned-cowboy drove hard right up until his death. He was buried at his home, *Po'o Kanaka*—"Man's Head."

Po'o kanaka also means "pansy flower." Purdy was the first to plant the flower on the Big Island, and the Hawaiians claimed that the blossom put them in mind of a person's head. It's possible today to still see a few Parker Ranch cowboys wearing pansy leis on their hats. Strangely, the flower is seldom seen at other places on the Island, where the *akulikuli* replaces it.

By 1830 King Kamehameha III had appointed Adams Kuakini as governor of the Island of Hawaii, and Kuakini took up residence at Waimea in connection with the taking of wild cattle. John Parker continued to round up, kill, and market the animals. It was at this time, with the king indebted to the extent of $3,500 to an American merchant named Pierce, that even more pressure was applied for the obtaining of more cattle. It necessitated that Parker have even more help in the handling of the stock which he had assembled on the lower ranges.

Knowhow was at a premium, and it was fortunate that the three celebrated Mexican-Spanish cowboys—Kossuth, Louzeida, and Ramon—had been brought over from the mainland to work the ranges and break Hawaiians into a more efficient way of handling cattle, horses, and all the equipment essential to the business. The newcomers first started working out of Hanaipoe on the slopes of Mauna Kea just twelve miles east of Waimea.

These vaquero arrivals wore low-crowned hats with wide brims, called sombreros. Around their necks—and sometimes the head—they wore a bright kerchief which they called a bandana. Their pants were baggy from the hips to the knees, but buttoned snugly from there down to the ankles. A knife strapped to the right leg gave a sinister touch. As for their footwear, they wore high-leather shoes with low heels. They looked very dashing when mounted in their Spanish-style saddles with the big horns and colorful shawls.

But it was the coiled lassos (lariats) which most caught the eyes of the Hawaiians—and the dexterity with which the *paniolos* employed them. These were made of rawhide, or sometimes horsehair. Tough, strong, and functional, the rawhide rope (*kaula ili* in Hawaiian) of the *paniolo* was as important to him as a sword is to a swordsman or a cannon to an artilleryman. One

big difference, however, is that the *paniolo* made his own imple-
ment. He worked with pride and ingenuity constructing it. The
finished product had to serve him well, an instrument in which
he could put his whole trust. Sometimes his very life depended
upon it.

First he selected a strong, perfect hide, then scraped off all
the hair—*koe i ka hulu*. In a spiral cutting from the very center
of the hide, he sliced a strip, from three-quarters of an inch to
a full inch thick, with a razor-sharp knife. Talent was essential
to cut evenly and true all the way. Upon finishing the cutting,
he divided the long strip into four even lengths. If he wished a
more elaborate lariat, he would braid eight strands. He generally used cattle fat to soften and oil the strips; he did this by
repeatedly running the strips through the oil in his hand. After
the strips were satisfactorily pliable and flexible, he braided
them into a single rope that felt snaky and alive, able to leap out
from its coil and strike true to its mark.

He furnished a loop at one end by affixing a metal ring to it;
at the other end of the rawhide rope he fashioned a tight, neat
knot. The length of the *kaula ili* was a matter of individual taste.
Some *paniolos* insisted on having it as long as 110 feet. Much
depended upon the kind of country the *paniolo* would be working in.

When completed and ready for use, the coiled *kaula ili* was
strapped to the *okuma*, or saddle horn, with a piece of leather
with a loop in it, which in turn was fastened to the saddle tree.
The piece of leather—the *kaula hoopaa*—which held the rope
was slipped through the coil several times, and the loop placed
over the saddle horn. However, when a *paniolo* was prepared to
use the rope at any undetermined time, the coil of *kaula ili* was
merely placed over the saddle horn for instant use. A typical
good *paniolo* needed his lasso the way he needed his next breath
—and he knew it. Today, only a few old-time *paniolos* still make
and work with the rawhide rope. The younger generation now
uses hemp and linen.

The Mexican vaqueros were excellent and patient teachers, and the eager-to-learn Hawaiians were equally excellent as students. They learned fast and well. The more they learned and the more adept they became, the more worth they were to John Palmer Parker. They soon developed the selfsame legerdemain with the lariat which the vaqueros had demonstrated. In time they became equally as good horsemen and cowpunchers.

As for the horses, the original animals were none too excellent to work with. They dated back to those which Captain Richard Cleveland gave to John Young, an adviser of King Kamehameha I, in 1803. Their progeny had been running wild on the slopes of Mauna Kea for too many years. They were small in stature, but powerfully strong, and their wildness took a lot of breaking. Those who knew them best referred to them as "Mauna Kea horses."

Much of the terrain—as now—was a challenge for any horse, trained or untrained. Deep gorges, lava-strewn ranges, deep crevasses in the volcanic formations, steep mountains, cactus-ridden regions, areas tangled with *kiawe* (pronounced kee-av-ee) and other thorny growths—all were there to thwart horse and rider, and still are.

Individually, the *paniolos* broke and trained their own mounts. Man and horse had to become one. This was done the tough, rough way—in open country. It was a case of simply catch your horse, heave the saddle up onto the *kau lio*, cinch it, and ride for your life!

The horses had to be right, and the *paniolos* skilled. The work to which these horses were put almost passes comprehension. They had to run over *a'a* (jagged lava, pronounced ah-ah) that could cut the average horse's feet to ribbons. They had to plow into the surf with riders on their back and struggling cattle lassoed to the rear of them. On the range, they had to come to grinding, stiff-legged halts when roped cattle were to be brought to a stop. They had to be nimble and alert to avoid the charge of stilleto-sharp horns. They had to be endowed with the stamina and strength of a Belgian stallion to withstand the grueling daily tests of chasing wild cattle or wild horses. The dust, heat, and grind of constantly herding stubborn and defiant horned animals was enough to break down anything but an outstanding horse and rider. And the dangers were ever-present.

Apropos of the importance of excellent horseflesh to the development of the cattle industry in those old *paniolo* days, Eben Low, *kamaaina* (long-time resident), former Hawaii state representative and a member of the Parker family, had this to say:

"In Hawaii, the particularly daring exploits of the cowboys in pursuit of the wild cattle through the dangerous and tricky mountains made the question of horses one of paramount importance.

"Animals with stamina, speed, intelligence and stout hearts were as necessary to a cowman as a good pair of legs to an Olympic runner, and many are the sagas that cattlemen will tell you of horses whose heroic deeds are forever written in the hearts of men to whom a horse is a friend to be admired and respected. Hawaii has had her full measure of great horses, and without them there would be no story of dashing devil-may-care horsemen."

In addition to the finely trained, intelligent horse and the cobra-striking lariat, the *paniolo* counted heavily upon another item, his saddle—a thing that was almost part of him. The old-time Parker Ranch saddle had no nails or tacks in it. It was hand-pegged, sewed, and the tree planed by hand. Ordinarily each *paniolo* constructed his own saddle at home and took great care in the building of it.

Today, however, Parker Ranch has its own saddle shop, run by John Kianiani Kauwe. He builds a saddle to his own fastidious taste. His father taught him the art of saddle-making many years ago. John turns out these handmade saddles for the whole ranch today—every one of them a work of art.

Making a Parker Ranch saddle requires long and careful work. Two sections of strong neleau wood are shaped and hand-planed into the foundation for the saddle tree. Both underboards are tightly covered with rawhide and hand-sewn with goat hide. The *okuma*, or pommel, is also made of a solid piece of wood. This *okuma* is then covered tightly with rawhide. Next, additional tough leather is added to the neck of it to withstand the friction and strain where the *paniolo* wraps his rope to halt a moving steer. Otherwise, the lariat could well burn grooves into the *okuma* and ultimately weaken it to the breaking point.

For expediency, the *okuma* is tacked temporarily to the underboards. Holes are then drilled through the two jutting ends of the *okuma* and the two sections of underboards, and pegged with neleau wood about a half-inch thick and four inches long. The wooden pegs are then knocked firmly into place. When the temporary tacks are pulled out, the *okuma* is pegged securely to the underboards.

Next comes the backboard, a hand-planed arced piece of wood covered with rawhide and hand-sewn with goat hide. After the backboard has been temporarily tacked to the two underboards, holes are drilled and the pieces hand-pegged into their proper places. Then, with the *okuma*, the underboards, and the backboard all assembled, the leather parts are added; that is, the underpiece of leather, then the back piece, stirrups, and other necessary parts. On occasion, a large sheet of leather, the *lala*, is placed over the whole saddle as a decoration. It serves no function other than serving as seat padding, but the old vaqueros often added them for decoration. Parker Ranch *paniolos* put their own leather markings in the way of identification on their saddles. The patterns of these markings are hand-stamped, very individual, and the men take rightful pride in them. Incidentally, the saddles constructed for "shipping"—that is, where the mounted horses had to swim into the surf to work cattle up to the dinghy—were made of very little leather; the salt water tended to rot the toughest of leather.

In this new era the Parker Ranch *paniolos* have, for the most part, made alterations in the saddle. It still has the general features and lines of the old vaquero saddle, but the horn, or pommel, is smaller. For purposes of the Hawaiian *paniolo*, this is an improvement.

Old-time *paniolos* will tell you that the Hawaiian cowboys had to learn many things through raw experience, rather than from the imported vaqueros. The reason was that even the Mexicans had not had to contend with such wild cattle in their own country. The steers in Mexico and the southwestern United States were, by comparison, much on the domesticated side. So the handling of this new brand of wild cattle took all the courage and finesse that a vaquero could muster. Top riding was mandatory; magic roping was a must. Each time a wild steer was lassoed, the horseman could well expect the animal to charge with its long knife-sharp horns.

Accustomed to this, the Hawaiian cowboys were fortified with this one advantage. In fact, in some circles it is said that once the Hawaiians learned the horsemanship and roping of the vaqueros, they became peerless in their work just because of their familiarity with the wild beasts and the terrain.

Despite the increased number of cowboys taking cattle and readying them for delivery, the numbers of cattle themselves continued to increase vastly. History tells us that in 1840, 5,000 hides were taken. Between the years 1845 and 1884, an average of 2,000 were exported annually. By 1846 there were an estimated 25,000 wild and 10,000 tame cattle on the Big Isle. Parker continued building his business, increasing his own herds. And, thanks to the fine early training of the imported vaqueros, Parker Ranch rightfully boasted of having the most efficient and hard-working cowpunchers the world had ever seen.

The work of a *paniolo* was a hard lot. His day began at dawn and seldom ended before sunset. His pay was minimal. He was in the saddle most of the day, and the work with feisty cattle was fraught with danger without letup. When he was through with his day's hard labor on the range, he had a thousand odd, but important, jobs to attend to. It was essential that he tend to his horse, and care for the saddle and tack which took the day's beating. His rawhide rope needed checking and repairing. There was generally wood to be chopped for his stove. Unless he had a wife, there was cooking to be done and a slew of household things to attend to. Often he spent his evening hours breaking in and training a spare horse. His extracurricular duties seemed manifold and endless. It was a hard, raw life, but the men were working in a paradise of a land with unbelievably good weather most of the time. The biggest virtue was that they were doing the thing they most wanted to do. In addition, John Parker was an understanding employer and dealt fairly with his men.

In their effort to track down the wild steers *(pipi)*, they depended much upon the sensitivity of their horses. In heavily brushed or forested areas, the horse often smelled or sensed the presence of concealed *pipi* before the rider did. The horse's ears and eyes would come alert and point out the direction of the quarry. The horses literally played the role of bird dogs.

Upon sighting the *pipi*, the *paniolo* would immediately dismount and quickly cinch up the saddle girth *(kaula opu)* in preparation for the hard work ahead. Remounted again, the *paniolo* would ride toward the animals with coiled lariat in hand and pick out the one he wanted to rope. He always preferred a bull, whose hide was generally finer and bigger. Sometimes there would be a mad chase as the whole herd would stampede away. But at other times it was a case of one or more of the bulls turning and charging at the horse. A *paniolo* had to be ready for any eventuality, and his mount had to be prepared to jump with a sudden scramble of haunches.

Where there was no immediate charge involved, the *paniolo* would single out the animal he wanted and work it toward a clearing where he could use his lariat freely, with no overhanging tree limbs or tall tangles to interfere with the accuracy of the throw. The heavy growths of mamane, ohia, and koa trees, which provided the wild cattle with regions of concealment, worked havoc with horse and rider. The alternative was to drive the wanted beast into one of the few clearings, called *kipuka* or *pa hu'a*. These were places well marked and named by the *paniolos*, and they drove their prey there as fast as possible before the animal could break away to again join the herd, or crash deeper into the heavy growth and escape.

It took a sure-footed horse, fast, strong, and smart. In addition, the *paniolo's* lassoing had to be a perfect sleight-of-hand bit. The instant the *pipi* was driven into the *kipuka*, the rider had to throw his loop with unerring accuracy before the animal could race across the clearing and disappear into the denseness on the other side. Good roping was of the essence, or the bull was lost.

If the throw was precise and the bull was lassoed, the *paniolo* swiftly took several turns of the rope on the horn of the saddle. His trained horse would come to a stiff-legged stop, and the lariat would cinch up and go stick-straight with the tension of the writhing bull on the other end. The saddle horn, the girth, the lasso—all would become taut and close to the breaking point as the strain hit its peak. Horse and rider had to be perfectly coordinated. If he failed in any of these departments, the rider might well find himself unhorsed—maybe even under the horse's belly and ludicrously tangled with the hanging saddle. There was always the grim possibility that the enraged bull would charge with lowered horns slashing like bayonets. Many a good horse was lost this way, and occasionally a *paniolo* paid with life or limb.

If the bull didn't charge, he would try desperately to disentangle himself from the strangling noose, for he was strictly, in the Hawaiian tongue, *eli ka lepo*—"mad like hell." This was always the moment of truth, for the *paniolo's* next move was to keep the lariat taut and work the bull over to a strong tree to cinch it around the trunk. When the animal was brought up against the tree and held there by the back-pulling horse, the *paniolo* would dismount and lash the bull's head close to the trunk with a short hand rope. Once the bull was firmly secured in this manner, the *paniolo* was free to get back into his saddle and search for another bull. This was repeated again and again until possibly eight or ten wild cattle were firmly tied to trees.

It was a long, dangerous day, but it was the *paniolo's* life, and at the end of the day there was usually a group of captive wild cattle tied in the various clearings. Dusty, weary, and sweaty, the *paniolos* would return to their headquarters, knowing that their biggest job was behind them.

On the following day the *paniolos* took tame bullocks out to the *kipukas*, tying them to the wild ones. Then, when the animals were securely paired up, the domesticated ones would lead the wild ones back to the pens at headquarters. This procedure worked extremely well except in instances when the *paniolos* occasionally found a dead animal still tied to a tree where it had broken its neck in trying to break loose. As crude as the method was, thousands of wild cattle were successfully caught and brought to the pens in this manner.

Two other methods were sometimes used, but they worked only when the wild bullocks were of a more tame and controllable type. One way was to wait for moonlit nights when the *pipi* came down in herds from the forest or higher regions to drink at the ponds. A pond at Waimea, called Makini, often attracted whole herds of wild cattle to its edges, where they slaked their thirst. It was a prime waiting place for the *paniolos* and often saved them from much riding through tangled, wooded regions where the cattle were difficult to find—and even harder to catch. One more way which sometimes worked, when the cattle were not too wild, was to take a whole herd of domesticated cattle up into an area of *pipi*, allow them to mingle with the wild ones in order to placate the latter, then work the entire herd—wild and tame—back down to the pens.

The life of the early Spanish-Mexican *paniolos* left its indelible mark on Parker Ranch, and much of it can be seen to this day. Its evidence abounds particularly in items which have to do with saddlery, handling of horses, cowboy raiment, and general riding accouterments. As far back as 1890, Curtis J. Lyons, an authority on Hawaiian affairs, read a paper to the Hawaiian Historical Society, telling of Spanish influences. Mr. Lyons wrote:

"At Waimea, Hawaii, on the high land plateau, there ranged the wild cattle descended from Vancouver's original importation, long-horned Spanish cattle like unto the modern Texas steer. At Waimea the Mexican Hispano-Indian found his home and occupation. He was called by the Hawaiian specifically: Huanu, Hoke, Hoakina, etc.; these names, of course, meaning Juan, José Joachim, etc. He had with him sometimes full-blooded Indians of Mexican origin, whom I saw in my boyhood. He was called generically: *Paniolo* or *Espagnol*, the words that nowadays mean 'cowboy.'

"He introduced the saddle in all its rich adornment of stamped bull-hide leather, and stirrups broad-winged. He brought the jingling spur with bells of hand-wrought steel. He brought the hair rope in strands of alternate black and white, and the hand-whirled wheel for turning it; also the hand-wrought bit—not so crude as it looked to be, and a necessity in bullock hunting. All this away back in the thirties, long before the birth of the modern cowboy.

"Do not I remember him well, this Spaniard Kossuth, Louzeida and Ramon—the red bandana handkerchief tied over his head under the broad flapping hat with rim upturned in front. Did not the serape (*poncho*, we always called it, and the name must have come from South America) commend itself to our common sense as a defense from rain? We adopted it, and the red silk sash in the bargain, and the leggings not buttoned.

"Last but not least, the lasso or lariat braided evenly and lovingly from four strands of well-chosen hide, then well-stretched and oiled, coiled in the same left hand, that with the little and third finger held the finely braided bridle rein. Mexican, too, this was, and Mexican the causing of the rein to bear on the horse's neck instead of to pull on the mouth. A more formidable weapon, this lasso, than revolver or Winchester. And no artist has yet mastered the problem of depicting the throwing of the lasso—not even the inimitable Frederick Remington.

"These Spaniards are the men that taught the Hawaiians the conquest of the wild herds of Mauna Kea; not tens, but hundreds of thousands, of skeletons have bestrewn the sides of that old mountain. They rode the descendants of the old Moorish horse—the tough bronco. . . .

"Mexican saddles, bits and bridles, spurs and pack saddles, were long a specialty of Waimea manufacture. The tan pit, the blacksmith's shop, the saddler's shop, and shoemakers, too, all flourished as home industries. Now, alas, no longer. The wire fence is limiting the size of the drive in the *hoohulu pipi* (roundup, the Americans call it). The merchant ship brings the cheap spur and inferior saddle for the degenerate *paniolo* of 1892; and so on. In short, the times are changed."

Although many jeeps, pickup trucks, heavy trucks and station wagons are seen in ranch operations at the Parker spread now, the *paniolo* is still the backbone of the herding, the roundups, the sorting, the many things which only the rider and his horse can do with utmost efficiency.

In time the *paniolos'* blood strains were mixed with the Hawaiians, the Caucasians, the Orientals, and others, and a hybrid man developed—the born cowhand. By the turn of the century there were men working the Parker Ranch who were the equal to the great range wranglers of any of the Western states.

Cowboy Jimmy Lindsey, when late in his eighties, told of his life in wrangling cattle on the Parker Ranch. He was born in Waimea in 1882 at a time when his grandparents still lived in a grass house, then known as a *hale pili*. He was born to the rawhide rope and rode his first roundup before he had entered his teens. By age fifteen he was a full-fledged horsebreaker and *paniolo*. He learned to know the fern jungles and plains the way he knew the back of his hand. He had a way with animals, both horses and cattle. Stooped and bowlegged from so many long, hard years in the saddle, he searched his memory and told of the hardships, dangers, and rewards of being a cowpuncher in those days. Being hurt by unbroken horses or wild steers was almost inevitable. Even his own brother, Tom, was killed on the slopes of Mauna Kea when his half-wild horse fell with him. They had been slaughtering cattle on the high flats.

Butcher Henry Hall of Honokaa purchased most of the Parker Ranch beef in those days, and Lindsey said it was "blood money" being paid for the animals. Getting the wild cattle into camp was no sinecure. Men were worn out in doing it; some were crippled; some lost their lives.

The foreman—known as the *luna*—would tell the men to bring enough blankets and food to live a few days in the forests and canyons and hunt for beeves. They would make their catches and bring them back to Waimea. The progeny of some of those men were to become rodeo men of the first order. One such man, Ikua Purdy, was born on Parker Ranch on Christmas Eve, 1874. He was practically born on a horse. His father had him riding before he could walk. Before he was in his teens Purdy was roping wild steers out on the range. By the time he had grown into a man he was a past master with rope, horse, and steer. Those who saw him work said it was legerdemain the way he'd make a rope hiss to its mark, the way he'd drop a steer or heifer, and the way he'd do his tying.

At rodeos, both in the Islands and on the mainland, he startled the throngs with some of his "black magic." He roped, threw, and tied wild steers in a fashion that left the onlookers gaping in awe. He had a gargantuan appetite for doing his job right, and set a shining example in riding and roping for the younger men coming up. He was a blending of fluid grace and raw power. He did everything a rodeo could demand of a man —and he did it in a lavish, flamboyant way.

Other fantastic Island cowhands became legendary in their trade. There was the Parker Ranch's Eben "Rawhide Ben" Low who—with only one hand!—beat the current world champion at his prime. Ben Low had lost his left hand in a roping accident years before, yet executed all the deft moves of a top cowhand as if he had no handicap whatsoever.

Today, old Island cowmen talk of other fantastically talented Parker Ranch hands, such as Eben Low's brother, John, and his half-brother, Archie Kaaua.

Another cowboy of heroic proportions was Jack Nae'a Purdy. The people of Kiholo, near Kawaihae, particularly knew and respected him for his courage and talent in every phase of cowpoking. They reminisce about how he would swim his horse out to the distant cattle steamers. When cattle occasionally broke loose from their lashings on the accompanying dinghy and panicked seaward, Jack Nae'a Purdy was the man who swam his horse out to retrieve them. On the roughest of terrain, in canyon or on lava slope, he was also extraordinary. His sheer riding and roping genius could survive sluicing storm, blasting heat, or high-mountain cold.

To this day all these challenges (except cattle-swimming) prevail on the Parker Ranch. Good riding, sound horses, top roping, and courageous men continue to be a must. Even the heavy, suffocating dust of the moving herds is still a threat to *paniolos*. Much of the ranch weather on the higher levels is crisp and misty in the nights and early mornings. Cattle droppings become damp, then the sun blazes as the day advances, and the prairie land dries out. When a strong, driving wind comes up, or herds of cattle are on the move, the droppings become mixed with dust and form a stinging element that blows into the eyes and nostrils of man and beast. The smarting of the eyes, nasal passages, and throat can be insufferable. Still, these range riders go at their chores. They are Parker men.

A Family and a Ranch

B y 1835 John Palmer Parker the First was a swarthy, gray-haired bull of a man with a weathered face. This was the year when he moved his family and belongings to Waimea where he would be more centrally located for distribution of his time and effort. Waimea was no more than an inland village on the farming plateau. He built a small home at Puuloa. This transplanted sailing ship man had become a great advocate of home and hearth.

He continued carrying out King Kamehameha III's wishes: slaughtering wild cattle and getting the beef, hides, and tallow to market. It was lucrative for King Kamehameha, but he, like Parker, wanted a better grade of beef. Parker knew that the only answer would be found in careful choosing of animals and in private breeding. He lived for the day when he could develop his own select herd on a large scale.

Waimea, the birthplace of the Parker Ranch, had a distinctive charm in the 1830s. Albert Lyons, the son of Reverend Lorenzo Lyons, who came there in 1832 and labored at his lonely mission station for fifty-four years, described it beautifully. In retrospect, he speaks nostalgically of Waimea (Waikoloa)" . . . the murmur of distant falls background for resonant voices coming from the great herds of semi-wild cattle that grazed on the plain—background also to the yells of the Hawaiian *paniolo* that so wildly galloped by." He speaks of "the rhythmic thud of tapa beating," and "a common thing to hear some aged native chanting old-time *olis.*" And lastly, "The visits of a *makamaka* [loved one] were sometimes the occasion of emotion that expressed itself in an abandon of wailing."

And, as quoted in Emma Lyons Doyle's fine history, *Makua Laiana*, Albert Lyons is quoted:

"Waimea [Waikoloa] was a place of solitude, but a solitude by no means voiceless. The hours were few in the 365 days of the year when there was not a 'sound going' in the mulberry trees. Normally the pliant boughs were strained and lashed by a northeast wind having the force of a full gale. The diapason of the weird music it made was the dominant fact of consciousness. Often for days at a time the wind was charged with fine drops of rain—Scotch mist we called it—and then its voice took on a fiercer, more uncompromising tone. This is the *'ua ki puu puu* of Waimea' [The rain that raises the goose flesh]. The epithet, like the local epithets of Homer, is the fierce impact of those minute raindrops driven by the violent wind gusts against unsheltered window panes that makes a wild music like that of a driving sleet storm in New England.

"During the winter months come westerly breezes, swaying backward the mulberry boughs to which the more prevalent trades have given a permanent set toward the west, adding to the aeolian music a new and distant note. Beginning with a lisping whisper it swells to an inarticulate outcry of protest. Only rarely does this west wind approach the force of a gale [a Kona storm], when the clashing together of the backward bent branches, and the snapping of twigs and boughs give to the music a martial motif. Great branches may finally be torn from trees which have withstood for decades the westward urge of the more violent trade winds."

Obviously, to Lyons, Waimea, in the heart of the Parker Ranch country, was a symphony of sound, at least in many respects. This was the Waimea plateau, then covered by a forest largely of the ohia lehua.

Archives contain a description of the cattle conditions of this region in those times. The writer of the article had visited the place at the time of Parker's struggle to establish his ranch. His description was printed in the *Sandwich Island Gazette* of September 10, 1836. It read:

"Waimea is a district of Kohala, one of the six great divisions of Hawaii, consisting principally of a large expanse of tableland, bounded on the north by the mountains of Kohala, on the south by the lofty Mauna Kea, easterly by the woody regions of Hamakua, and on the west stretches northwest of Kawaihae to some large kou trees—near Kiholo where runs the line of separation between Kohala and Kona. . . . The country is abandoned to the wild cattle which are large and numerous, and have afforded no inconsiderable revenue to the chiefs for some years past; they are scattered about in herds enjoying the fine pastures which the plains afford. At Lihue and at other places, bullock-catchers are stationed, who have pens as they are styled, for catching bullocks at different places on the foot of Mauna Kea, on the southern side of the plain. They are built of strong posts of hard wood, with crossbars of the same, strongly lashed together with strips of rawhide; they are of various dimensions. From the entrance of the pen are two diverging fences built of the same materials, extending from a quarter to half a mile in length. Into this funnel, a herd of wild cattle are driven by a number of horsemen, and propelled on until they enter the pen—the entrance of which is immediately closed. A man on horseback then enters the pen, with no other weapons that his knife and a lasso, singles out those which he requires, throws him down, and either has him dragged to another pen, or dispatches him instantly. Those which are intended to be tamed are fastened to a post and fed until they quietly allow the approach of their keeper; they are then tied by thongs of hide to the horns of a tame one, and suffered to go at large; by the time the thongs chafe off they are supposed to be sufficiently domesticated.

"It is difficult to conceive a situation of greater danger than that of the bullock-catcher when he rides into the pen amidst a herd of wild bulls. Their enormous size, savage disposition, activity and strength, seem to preclude the possibility of his escaping with his life—but habit destroys fear. The men here frequently ride carelessly in, irritate the already savage beasts, laugh merrily at their furious assaults, while with watchful eye and well disciplined horse, they nimbly evade them, and as they madly rush by them aptly throw the noose over their heads and by a few skillful evolutions of the horse entangle their legs with the lasso and cast them bellowing to the earth. One or more assistants instantly seize a hind leg, the tail, or a horn, and the animal is either bound or butchered with facility.

"These bullocks are the offspring of those left here by Vancouver. They are found grazing in very large herds on the sides of the mountains. Within the last few years many thousands have been caught. The bulls are generally killed for their hide and tallow, the flesh is generally wasted, part of the cows are slain, but their flesh is either eaten or jerked for the Oahu market, or packed in barrels for ship use; the rest of the cows and calves are sent by shiploads to Honolulu. Some oxen are broken in after the Spanish fashion to draw immense loads in rude cars adapted to the roughness of the country and badness of the roads.

"Those parts of the plain adjoining Hamakua are better wooded, having a parklike appearance, with numerous herds of wild cattle and many wild boars, which are either caught in pit falls, shot or speared by the natives. Higher up the mountain the timber increases in size, being interspersed with Ohia [*Eugenia*], Koa [*Acasia falenia*] and Naiho [*Myoporum Tenue folium*].

"The western part of the district remains to be noticed. This consists of a gradual descent of about 10 miles to the seaside. It is entirely composed of an uneven rocky waste, covered with long grass. This barren tract is untenanted and uncultivated. Rain seldom falls here and, besides the grass, nothing is seen to vary the monotony until you approach the coast, when the eye is only relieved by the yellow blossoms of the Nohu [*Tribulus*].

A road has lately been made from the plain to Kawaihae by clearing away the stones and covering the surface with long grass. This is the work of convicted offenders against the laws. The road terminates at Kawaihae near a large temple built by Kamehameha the First—of which more hereafter. There is an anchorage for vessels and a harbour for small craft. At this place and at Puako, about 2 miles to the south, are shipped off the cattle and other produce of Waimea for Honolulu. The anchorage, however, is bad, and vessels are frequently blown off by the *mumuke*, or strong northeast wind."

Such was the region into which John Parker moved his home. It was a rough country in which to make a living, but he had come into it undaunted and with courage high. He had a habit of quoting an old Arabian proverb: "He who has health has hope, and he who has hope has everything." It was a creed he lived by.

A second child was born to the John Parkers in 1827. Eight years had elapsed since the birth of little Mary Ann Kaulalani Parker. This time it was a boy, and they named him John Palmer Parker II; his Hawaiian name was Kamaikaaloa Kalanioku— "Keone Paka" the Hawaiians called him—and he brought a new dimension into the Parkers' lives. He was loved by all who knew him.

He was especially important to Kipikane, for, during those eight barren years, she had begun to grieve deeply, afraid that she could not produce a man-child as an heir for her husband. Now her life was full.

John Parker early began teaching the youngster everything about ranch life. The two were close, and as time went by Parker taught the boy all the pedestrian chores of cattle ranching, from making butter to milking cows and throwing a lasso.

John Parker II grew into manhood and married a Hawaiian girl by the name of Hanai. Her ancestors were bond slaves— belonging to the kauwa, those "untouchables" who, in the past, had been in bondage and often selected for human sacrifice.

Young John's mother and his Hawaiian relatives were very much against his marrying this girl, for it was felt he was marrying below his class. However, the marriage was a happy and lasting one.

John's father built a new home at Mana for the newlyweds. He set up a koa house a few feet from his own original koa home, and it was named *Kapuai Kahi*—meaning "one square foot." It was most comfortable for those times, with a sitting room or parlor, one bedroom, a dining room, a kitchen, and a storeroom. A spacious koa-lined attic, a small koa *lanai* (porch), *pahua* mats, and calico-curtained windows made the koa house a tidy, comprehensive home.

Hanai was a picturesque and loved woman. She became renowned for many things, among them her habit of riding horseback with a gay *pa-u* flowing, and carrying a round sewing box just in front of her saddle. Young John took great pride in her, and it is told how he used to point at her astride the horse, saying, "*Nani kuu wahine!*" (My wife is beautiful!).

Due to the *alii* blood flowing through young John's veins, and the *kauwa* blood in Hanai's, the natives predicted dire things for the baby, which Hanai was soon carrying. They prophesied that the disparity in blood class was too great and that the child would not live long. They also predicted that no other children would come of the marriage. They were right on both counts, for the infant (Samuel) lived less than a year—and the marriage never produced a second child.

Although Hanai spoke only Hawaiian, she oddly did not encourage her own people to visit her in her home. She had become a Christian woman, and it was common to hear her saying the Lord's Prayer aloud in her room before she retired each night. If she had any major fault, it was her "saving" to the point of being penurious. She was known to save scraps of food until spoilage had set in. Some of her compulsive penuriousness might be attributed to the fact that she came from a long line of very poor people.

On the other hand, in later years she idolized her nephew by marriage, Samuel Parker, and refused him nothing. In making his linen suits for him when he was attending Punahou School on Oahu, she had a habit of sewing ten-dollar gold pieces into the lining of each coat. She did this because his grandfather allowed him only twenty-five cents a week for spending money. She was enormously clever with sewing for her husband and nephews, but was talkative, outgoing, and witty as well. She had a habit of greeting everyone by his or her Hawaiian name, often throwing in a little provocative Hawaiian chant to please the visitor. She possessed a good figure and affected large, gorgeous prints in her colored *muumuus.*

She was a good wife for John Parker II and worked with him during the days of establishing the Parker Ranch. As John Palmer Parker I grew older, his son, John, gradually took over more and more of the management of the ranch.

Records reveal that during the younger John's reign, he usually rounded up the wild cattle from the high slopes and deep canyons, and drove them to market for slaughter or shipping in lieu of thinning out the herds of semitamed cattle which ranged his Waimea plains. He seemed to delight in seeing the thousands of cattle constantly grazing in the area between Waimea and Mana. Maybe it was the sense of security which the sight gave him. True, they were not the blooded Herefords which so dot the Parker Ranch today, but to John II they were a reassuring and beautiful sight. They were, of course, actually the descendants of the Mexican longhorn cattle which Captain Vancouver had first introduced to the Islands so many years back. For John II, what they lacked in breeding they made up for in numbers.

However, in later years when Parker delegated one Paul Jarrett as manager of the ranch, the local herds—"John's pets," as they were often called—were swept away to market because they were easier to handle than the bush cattle. They were also in better condition as salable beef and consequently commanded bigger prices.

Within two years after John Parker II's birth, a second son,

Ebenezer, was born to Kipikane and John Parker. So now, in 1829, the Parkers had three heirs. Ebenezer, along with John II, became the closest companions of their father. This second son was named Eben. He was a particularly handsome boy and was made much over.

By the age of seventeen, Eben was beautifully built: six feet, four inches in height; lean, tall, and lithe. He had the imperial physique of an Hawaiian chief, and the gift of laughter. He was a top rider and fearless hunter. He and his brother accompanied their father and the *paniolos* on wild steer hunting and wild boar shooting expeditions.

Eben's short, but active, life was crammed with color, romance, love—and tragedy. Lusty, vital, and possessed of huge enthusiasms, Eben did everything in a carefree and relaxed way. He always, except in one instance, wore a broad smile.

It happens that those who knew him best realized that, for a while as a young man, his handsomeness and winning personality often led him into countless involvements with the *wahines* (females). For him, every day was like New Year's Eve. The *wahines* found he had an electric smile and muscles like the sinews of an ox's thigh. One member of the Parker family once wrote authoritatively: "Eben developed into a wild sort of fellow, crazy about women, and the natives encouraged it against his parents' approval—and oftimes without their knowledge." Much of the time he was obviously like a sailor on a spree; he had to have every parrot that was on sale on every waterfront.

Eben had given so much of himself to so many women, that he felt he could not possibly give all of himself to any one person. He was to find himself wrong on this count.

A paradoxical change came into Eben's life, and it stemmed from a bit of mere hearsay. One day a man from Maui arrived at the Parker Ranch, and he had great praise for a very beautiful girl on Maui who was being groomed as a *wahine kapu* (virgin) for the future wife of a Hana Maui chief. "Her beauty catches the breath," Eben was told.

The description of her rare loveliness, plus the fact that she was taboo and inviolate—here was a challenge to the young scion of the Parkers. Eben, the incurable romantic, had had his way with so many beautiful woman over the years that he was forever raising his sights for more exquisite game. Now he would sail to Maui to see this entrancing personality. A sacred individual? This he must see for himself and try his wiles on her. Like all Don Juans, he intended to keep his heart free—but he would have this girl!

It has been authenticated by several sources that he boarded a small vessel, went to Maui, and arrived at the gate of the home where the girl was staying in Hana. Identifying her by the description imprinted on his mind, he saw her among others under a pandanus tree in a courtyard. She was sitting on a small *makaloa* mat, and those around her were weaving *hala leis* (pandanus wreaths). It was obvious that the girl had just come in from a swim in the sea, for her slim, glistening body sparkled as though studded with diamonds, and the raven hair that fell down her back was shimmering-moist. She wore a red *hala* lei on her head, and her skin was clear olive.

Eben stood, transfixed. He was later to tell that he had never seen a girl of such heart-stopping beauty, nor had he ever before been so enchanted. Suddenly her luminous black eyes lifted and took in this tall stranger with the whipcord pants, the Wellington boots, felt hat with the rosebud lei, and silk kerchief around his neck. The look of royalty and intelligence in her face startled Ebenezer. This was truly a taboo girl, not to be touched, not to be violated—meant only for the possession of the *alii*. She was so winsome that Eben could not withdraw his gaze. Yet he knew he had no right to invade her privacy this way, nor was he fulfilling the role of gentleman by gaping at her in so rude a manner. Pride, shame, and desire fought a three-way battle within him. He detested his own impertinence. After all, he was supposed to be a man of quality. Embarrassed, he turned to go.

At his retreat, the girl quickly rose with liquid grace and called, "*Mai! Mai!*" (Come! Come!) "*Komo mai e ka malihini!*"

(Come in, stranger!) She motioned for him to return. Eben slowed his step, hesitantly turned, and looked back over his shoulder, noticing the dismay on the faces of her friends and retainers. To the *aliis*, this social aggressiveness was in the worst of taste. She quietly insisted that he sit by her on her taboo mat —an unheard-of thing in Polynesian tradition.

They sat, and he began to learn about her; and she about him. In a whispery, rich voice, she told him that her name was Kilia (Celia) and that she was pledged to the hand of a certain chief of Maui. She described the kind of training which she was undergoing and the care with which her peers were devoting to her grooming. He told her of his own position in life on the vast Parker estate. She had ordered food, and together they ate poi from her taboo calabash—another alarming digression from the ways of the old *alii*.

They were in the midst of the meal and eagerly talking when Kilia's grandfather appeared, in a finely made tapa cloak. His aristocratic but stiff manner augured no good for either of these two young people. The old chief's brows knitted, and, in a deep, booming voice, he demanded of his granddaughter, "*O wai keia mahaoi hapa haole?*" (Who is this bold half-white?)

Eben quickly broke in with, "I am the son of John Parker of Waimea, Hawaii."

Recognition flashed across the coppery face of the older man; he well knew Kipikane's white husband—the rancher with the tremendous acreage, the thousands of cattle, and reputation for lavish hospitality. He also knew that the senior Parker was a relative and had been a personal friend to the late King Kamehameha the Great. The young couple was in the middle of a repast, and it is an old Polynesian custom to observe the rule of never disturbing a guest who is eating in one's home. Hawaiian etiquette won out, and the grandfather resigned himself to permitting Eben to be reseated.

Much talk followed, with all three partaking of the poi and discussing things freely. One thing was certain, however, and that was that the grandfather was adamant about Kilia being betrothed to the *alii* chief to whom she was promised. He said so in a voice like a rusty chain.

It was suddenly too late for Eben to make the boat which would take him back to Hawaii. He would have to leave on the morrow, so he was invited to remain overnight as a guest. He accepted, spent more time with Kilia and her grandparents, and became even more infatuated with her.

In the late hours of the evening Eben proposed marriage to Kilia. He also talked to the grandfather about it, but was spurned by the latter. As for Kilia, she did not know how to abrogate her arrangement with the chief whom she was pledged to marry. Her regard for Eben seemed as great as his regard for her. The night wore on, and Eben was able to have an even longer private talk with the girl. The moon rode at anchor in the sky, and the talk was deep and sober. Eben found something new about himself—something prideful and heretofore un-mined. Her proposed marriage was still somewhere in the distant future, and she said she was going to first come to Hawaii to pay a visit to her parents. Would Eben be at Waiapuka to meet her? Yes, he would; on his honor, he would.

In the morning Eben again talked with her grandfather, the chief, who suggested that Eben discuss his marriage desires with his own parents. "Maybe this love you speak of," he said, "is only a passing fancy. Take more time to think about it. You are a young man."

Eben left, suspecting—and rightly—that the old man simply wanted to push through the *alii* marriage without interference. Eben returned to the Big Isle and home.

In line with Kilia's suggestion that he watch the channel for her crossing, he spent much time at Waiapuka, gazing seaward from the cliffs in hope that he might see a great canoe coming in from the horizon across Alenuihaha Channel. Morning after morning he would arrive there as the sun came up, brilliant on the ocean. He waited for weeks and tried to go on trusting.

Then one day when the afternoon was waning, Eben spotted two heavily laden outrigger canoes in the distance where the winds spawn the swells. They were making their way shoreward. The first canoe was carrying Kilia and her people; the second one, also paddled by her retainers, was heavy with her calabashes, tapas, mats, and other personal belongings. But his eyes were transfixed on Kilia herself. She was ravishing in bright silks, and the feather wreaths against her coal-black hair gave her the regal touch that so belonged to her. She was queenly in carriage, gentle in manner.

Eben married his lovely *wahine kapu*, and she was welcomed wholly and royally by his parents. *"Kakou keikimahine!"* (Our daughter!) exclaimed Kipikane Parker as she hugged Kilia after the ceremony. The senior John Parker, too, embraced the girl and wished the newlyweds all the best things of life.

Eben proved to be a one-woman man from the time he first met and wooed Kilia. Kilia, too, was absolute in her fidelity and devotion toward her vows and her man. Kilia was not only Eben's wife, but also his special friend. Mutual worship was their tie, and their principal bond laughter.

John Palmer Parker I, patriarch of the expanding estate, furnished the newlyweds with a home by adding three rooms and a *lanai* to the structure at Mana. The Mana *hale* was beginning to develop into a veritable complex. In time, Eben and Kilia had four children—Mary Kaulalani Parker II, Ebenezer Parker II (who died at ten years of age), Samuel Parker, and Nancy Parker.

And this is what the founder of the ranch wanted—all the family together—children, grandchildren, and in-laws. As for work, there was much to do on the big ranch, with the old man's sons, Eben and John, carrying much of the load. Mary Ann and her husband, Waipa, also lived at Mana and took their share of responsibility. The whole place was a going, growing, expanding cattle kingdom.

Then the first great grief struck the Parker family: Ebenezer died suddenly in a grotesque way. While eating plover, he accidentally swallowed a sharp bone and it worked its way into his intestines and killed him. It was March 22, 1855. He was twenty-six years of age.

Kipikane and John Parker were shattered by the loss. Their boy had died so suddenly, in full stride, and the tragedy marked their souls. In truth, Eben's death breached John Parker's defenses. He aged rapidly.

The loss of Eben was a traumatic experience for Kilia, who loved him so desperately. Her mourning for him was practically psychotic. Her eyes became wells of sorrow. For months she wore his undershirt—the last thing that had touched his body at the time of his death. She could not be consoled, and for days and nights she slept in a tent which she had erected in the Mana graveyard where he was buried. She still had the taboo calabash from which they had first eaten together on Maui, and for many months she would not remove the remnant of poi that was still at the bottom of it. It was the last of something the two of them had shared, and her grief was so deep that she would not part with it. She even put new poi on top of it and partook of it with the feeling that she was again sharing food with the man she so loved in life.

In her deep depression, Kilia finally moved north to Kohala to be with her own parents. In her continued grief, she took to camping high on brooding Kohala Mountain with her people; and there, trancelike, she would gaze out across the land to where the Mana grave plot held her Eben in his final sleep. At night her people would light a fire for warmth against the high, chill mountain air. And there Kilia would sit, looking up at the stars through the wind-driven clouds over Mauna Kea.

Old John Parker I noticed the distant flame in the night, and when he learned from Kipikane what it was, he sent one of his men with an extra horse to bring Kilia back to Mana. The rider was successful in coaxing Kilia down from the mountainside, but she rode directly to the cemetery and threw herself upon Eben's grave. John and Kipikane didn't even know she was back

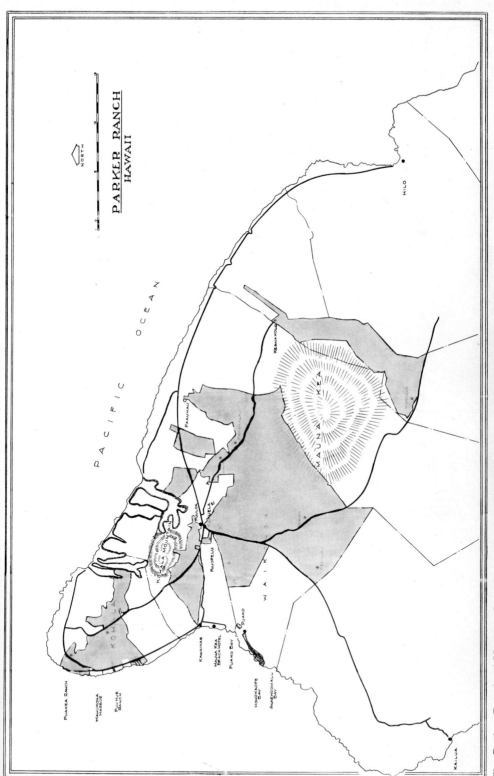

The Parker Ranch of Hawaii. Gray areas show the extent of the current ranch lands.

Ebenezer Parker, John Palmer Parker's second son

John Palmer Parker I

John Palmer Parker's home at Waimea

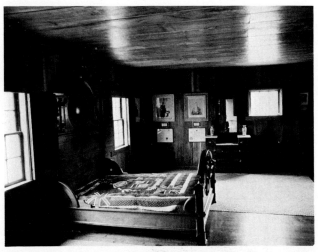

The bedroom from
John Parker's first home,
with all the original wood,
furniture, and fixtures.

The Parker family graveyard at Mana.

The Old Parker Ranch store

Colonel Sam Parker,
Princess Luka (Ruth)
Keelikolani and John Adams
Cummins. The men are
wearing butterfly feather
capes and holding kahilis.

Harriet Napela Parker,
the wife of Sam Parker

(Left) King Kalakaua, Jack Low, Sam Parker, and Eben Low;
(right) Harriet and Sam Parker's daughters, Eva and Helen

Sam Parker in middle age

Colonel Sam Parker's home at Kawaihae

The old-time *paniolos* on the range

until her riderless horse showed up at the gate. They went immediately to the private family graveyard and found her, still prostrate in her loneliness.

They managed to get her home again to Mana where they loved and cherished her, as only the elder Parkers knew how. They assisted her in the rearing of her four children and worked steadfastly at the problem of lessening her grief. It took time, but Kilia came somewhat out of her trauma, and, surprisingly, she was still beautiful, so much so that many men sought her hand in marriage. But she was still in love with Eben.

Among the men who sought the young widow's hand in marriage was a Mr. King. He came with excellent credentials, and John Parker I felt it could be a good marriage for his daughter-in-law. It could, he felt, prove therapeutic, for Kilia had gone again into a state of withdrawal. He advised her to accept Mr. King's proposal. Although Kilia felt no love for this man, she went through with the marriage and bore him two children, Willy and Mary King.

Six years after Ebenezer's death, Kilia was in Kohala when a great longing swept over her to revisit Hana Maui where her love affair with him had begun. She was only twenty-seven, but already living in the past. She wanted to see again her mother's people and some of the high chiefs from whom she was descended.

Although the wind was strong and inclement weather threatened, she prepared for the canoe passage across the channel to Maui. She wanted to go in the same manner which had brought her to Eben in the first place. With the weather worsening, everyone advised strongly against the voyage. But she was persistent and distraught—and possibly possessed by a death wish. On February 16, 1861, she departed Hawaii's shore with some of her people aboard a large canoe. She was last reported by those who saw her off as being chapel-silent. It was said that she stared seaward, and her mouth, full and delicately carved, was infinitely sad.

The sea became laced with white horses shortly after they

left the beach. They had not been long seaborne before the wind and water became a raging, living thing, striving to drag them down. The canoe and all on board were lost and never heard of again.

Those who knew Kilia best always insisted that she simply had not wanted to go on living. John Parker Senior had a tombstone erected in the Mana graveyard in memory of Kilia. It read starkly:

KILIA, WIFE OF EBENEZER PARKER

LOST IN THE PASSAGE BETWEEN MAUI

AND HAWAII FEB. 16TH, 1861

AGE 27 YEARS

The Joys and Toils

of Building

To ACQUIRE land that he could call his own had early been John Parker's basic target. He had been the first to see that the old cattle-hunting methods would give way to permanent ranching facilities and domesticated herds. Widespread killing of wild cattle had continued, despite a new taboo put upon the practice. Poaching and illegal cattle killing had become the order of the day for many people. The result was that the wild cattle population had sunk to a new low, and only domesticated cattle could begin to fill the gap.

At this point others, too, saw the danger. Pressure consequently arose from many *haoles*, who sought the aid of Kamehameha III. They sought a revision of land tenure in the Hawaiian kingdom, and the government ultimately saw the wisdom of such a move. On December 10, 1845, it took the first step in the direction of legalizing the absolute private ownership of land. The government instituted it by creating the Board of Commissioners to Quiet Land Titles. One of the stipulations emphasized by this Commission was that all claims for land had to be filed on or before February 14, 1848. Otherwise, interest in the land would be forfeited to the government.

John Parker had already filed his claim with the Commission on July 16, 1845, with this declaration: "I have made all preparations to build a small wooden house . . . if it is agreeable to you that I should have a small piece of land for my home lot in that lonesome desert."

Parker and a partner had been operating on lands in the foothills at the base of Mauna Kea, and their lease was to expire December 31, 1845. Time was running out, and Parker was determined to obtain lands in this region in order to continue his ranching venture.

By 1847, Parker's direct approach succeeded, for Kamehameha III agreed to grant him two acres of his own selection. The monarch accepted a mere ten dollars as a token of good faith—and, in a sense, the Parker Ranch was born at that moment. It was a small beginning for an ambition-ridden man like Parker, but the pioneer calculated that it would be better to light one candle than to curse the darkness. The small parcel of land was deeded to him in Royal Grant No. 7, dated January 14, 1847.

In truth, John Parker was seeking to work more and more on his own instead of being a functionary for the king. He wanted to depend less upon serving the sovereign as a cattle and produce supplier, to be more his own man, to build his own herd, to own his own land. He used to murmur quietly among his friends, "A man looks at himself, and he decides to do better." This was the heart of his credo.

Parker turned immediately to improving the property and making a home there that would be lasting. He was fortunate in having many strong and willing backs to help him, for Kipikane had brought as her dowry a retinue of servants who were loyal workers.

To replace his first home there, which was a mere temporary shack of *pili* grass and *ohia* bark, Parker started groundwork for the construction of a more permanent home. He built saw pits for the cutting of heavy koa wood which would give him a solid, weatherproof, almost indestructible, house. Soon construction was under way.

As always, he built well and sturdily. The foundations of the structure were of stone; the floors, walls, stairs, and ceiling of solid, everlasting koa wood. Constructed without benefit of lathes, power saws, or any modern equipment, the project was slow and laborious, but the structure took form and became a weatherproof, lasting, and, for those times, comfortable little home.

The place became the embryo for the rapidly developing ranch. Parker had additional koa houses built adjacent to the Mana place for his many lieutenants and workers and their families. It wasn't long before the nearby forest area was dotted with homes and bunkhouses. The enterprise thrived and expanded, for this was a rich land with unlimited potential. Parker's dreams were already taking tangible shape, a project which he could see and touch and work with.

An exact replica of that original wooden Mana house stands today under the slashing rains and whistling gales that sometimes sweep across Mauna Kea's slopes. This Mana house, now called the "Family Museum," is an exact restoration built at Mana and used by Samuel Parker. It stands quietly, simply, austere. It tries for no elegance or pomp, and hasn't even a *lanai* to indicate easier days. But it is where the huge Parker Ranch empire began.

The museum structure can be seen today with its koa floors, walls, and ceilings still shining. Gifts and mementos from long-gone people are hung on the walls or placed on stands and tables for the eye of the interested. There are many portraits of the succeeding ranch owners and their loved ones. They remind viewers that this is a ranch empire carved by much work, much hardship, and much faith. The men are portrayed as resolute, practical, and far-sighted individuals. Their wives, Hawaiian for the most part, appear gentle and trusting—fit mates for men who dreamed big dreams and planned mighty projects.

The place is rife with memoried things. Every item on wall, table, shelf, or in case challenges the imagination. One faded letter alone can hold your attention for minutes; a yellowed sheet of paper with a written note stops you and makes you wonder if the Islands would be any different today had the missionaries not arrived in the first quarter of the nineteenth century to save the souls of the so-called savages. A letter under glass is dated April 7, 1820, and is scrawled in a careful, almost childish hand. It was written by the missionary Reverend Bingham aboard the sailing brig *Thaddeus* and addressed to John Parker. It begs for help for the missionary cause, stating in part: "Six American gentlemen and their wives have arrived in Hawaii to diffuse the blessings of science, of civilization and Christianity in these isles of the sea." Today some people will tell you that only scars were left by the missionaries; others will insist vehemently that only good came of the arrival of these men of the cloth.

John Parker cleared more land for his truck gardening and erected stone walls and wooden corrals for his now semidomesticated cattle. He and his men dug cisterns for the storage of precious rain water.

Probably no better or truer pictures of those early times could be painted than that found in a letter written about forty years ago by Mary Low, the great-granddaughter of John Parker:

"John Palmer Parker I and wife, Kipikane, always lived like *aliis* [chiefs]. She had her retinue of servants, and he had his. It was below the koa forest of Hanaipoi that the saw pits were dug in the land known as Makahalau where the purebred bulls and cows are now penned up. This became the great center for koa work, cutting down of trees, selecting the best to be sawn up into lumber through the saw pits, the piling up of koa lumber on hilly ground so that the air could get between the boards and season the wood. There was so much lumber piled up in this section that the natives called the place *Palihooukapapa* [Hill of piling lumber].

"In the meantime at Mana, two underground cisterns were dug and plastered around for water, their roofs were of slate.

The dairy was also built, and it, too, had a slate roof. Next, the cornerstone was laid for a story-and-a-half dwelling house for Parker and family.

"Reverend Lyons of Waimea came up to dedicate it. Under the cornerstone was laid a Bible, a loaf of bread, an ear of corn, money, and newspaper of the time. This house was named *Mana Hale*, or 'Mana Hall.' The ground floor had four bedrooms, a large hall, dining room, kitchen, pantry and a closed-in porch, while the upper story had three rooms. Everything in and out of this house, even to the nails, was of koa grown on Parker lands, and sawn up in his saw pits.

"It was a very busy time as he had much to superintend and do to get comfortably settled. He also built a small stone house for storage of meat, etc.; also a saddle room and a roofed-in large shed for ploughs, ox or bullock wagons, etc. Parker also had men working on the servants' quarters. Work on all these buildings progressed very fast for the Master John was a kind man. His servants were numerous, and they were grateful to be paid in clothes and food.

"In those days they knew not the value of money. The Hawaiians of those days that appreciated money were those that went away in sailing vessels to other lands. All Parker's men had blue denims for everyday wear, and brown denims for Sundays. Women had dresses—*muumuus* [chemise]—given them. All were supplied with warm coats, blankets, towels, and wash soap.

"Parker was a great farmer! It is known of him that his foresight in feeding his establishment [household] and all laborers and retainers, with their families living under him were always provided for. This was done by planting, in their season, patches of dry land taro, Irish and sweet potato vegetables of all sorts.

"While busy at the saw pits, his men knew he was feeling anxious to find time to have a stone wall built so as to plough the land for planting. So one evening at five P.M. after the day's work and Parker had gone home for the day, the men took it upon themselves to build this wall and finished it that same evening as the evening star was seen in the sky. So the natives named this pen *Kau ka hoku* (The star is risen). Parker appreciated this thought of his men and had the place ploughed up next day and the seeds planted.

"Parker raised, besides cattle and sheep, turkeys, chickens and tame pigs. He was the first man in the Islands to import the quail and dandelion. Parker was a crack shot and kept his table bountifully supplied with plover and other game. In time his chickens and turkeys multiplied so that they went wild all through the forest.

"When a bullock or sheep was killed, no part of it was wasted. Tripe, liver, kidney, tongue, tail and brains, besides all choice cuts, were for the boss's table. Tallow was used in making soap, glue was made from the hoofs, and the hide made into ropes and rugs. All unused bones, etc. were made into bone meal for the vegetable plants. Also all taro peel was saved for manuring.

"Parker often made sausages from pigs, and was very fond of pickled pigs' feet, and head cheese which he spiced well with herbs planted specially for this purpose. He made use also of the plant life growing in the forest surrounding his home. All mattresses and pillows were made of *pulu* (a silky, soft substance from the tree fern).

"His family and retainers used Hawaiian herbs for medicine. They drank tea made from the *kokoolau* plant, a shrub. Wild strawberries and *pohas* when in season were used plentifully at their table. Also the frond of the fern *hoio*, which boiled and sprinkled with *kukui* nut, makes a good vegetable dish—the Hawaiians liking it raw as well with raw shrimps. He was exceptionally fond of every part of the taro leaves *(luau)* and the taro flowers *(haha)*—all fine vegetables when cooked. He cultivated Hawaiian *pia* [starch] for clothes and eating as well. The *pala* [yam] he relished roasted.

"All charcoal for ironing or for broiling purposes was made

in the forest out of a hard-dried *mamane* wood by baking in an *imu* [underground oven of hot stones]—the same as pigs are cooked. Only to make charcoal, the oven is not opened until a week after. Charcoal making days were always picnicking days for all families. For lunch in the woods was a feast of wild game and pig broiled over hot coals with roasted potato, taro, corn on the cob, eggs cooked in hot ashes, etc.

"Yes, the Parkers lived high, for everything was handed to them from nature's wonderful supply, and it is said Parker always had a peanut patch, and he and Kipikane ate roasted peanuts around the fireplace on cold nights while Kapuaa, her brother, would *oli* [chant] the names and histories of *allis* [chiefs] and chant also their own line of chief descent.

"They had no fireplace, really, but when nights were real cold at Mana, a large washtub half filled with ashes was brought in with a lot of charcoal burning hot on it, and they sat around the tub and got warmed up. Parker usually put a piece of dried sandalwood on the coals to perfume the room.

"Every Sunday Parker held church service in the large hall of Mana Hale. A *kouk* shell was blown to summon everyone. Each person was checked at the door to see if clean and properly clothed; otherwise they were made to clean up and return as quickly as possible properly washed and clothed. Parker read the services. He gave a sermon and they all sang hymns. Once a month Reverend Lyons of Waimea held the service at Mana. Parker and wife led the true patriarchal life. Parker was a cosmopolitan, enjoyed an evening of Hawaiian chants. His wife's brother was famous at it and entertained many of their friends that came to the ranch with old Hawaiian music and dancing.

"By energetic work Parker made a considerable fortune. Some of the land purchased from the King was paid for in butter by Parker. He possessed a fund of curious details about the customs and manners of the natives. He often spoke of Kamehameha I, the Conqueror. As a narrator, Parker had a peculiar charm. His stories were told without any pretensions and were interspersed with fragments of native chants, phrases and proverbs. He could chant very well."

John Parker had a way with him and he could always cast a glow over commonplace things. In the evenings he would tell his stories. His rich, resonant voice carried along the narrative, giving it tempo and vividness. Many sources tell us this. But mounting affluence never lessened his love of the land and all that went with it. To him the smell of the paddocks, the stables, the harness, the horse between his knees, was a scent fine as an orchard valley and sweet as summer.

Parker was an emotional man with a pioneer's sense of adventure. He made a religion of self-reliance. There was always humor and good talk around John Parker. He was a deep man, who believed in friendship, whose life was lit by love for his wife and his children. His philosophy was always homespun as a rag rug, as honest as a country doctor's. He always built everything with tomorrow in mind. He buried under the cornerstone of "Mana Hale" things which he thought would be of interest to posterity.

Parker was a quiet, nondrinking man who had to deal with many hard-drinking sea captains, merchantmen, tradesmen, and cattlemen, but he remained a teetotaler himself. He read the Bible daily, and reading it to his family was one of his delights. In preparation for the Sunday services, the womenfolk at Mana Hale would take *kukui* nut oil and polish the floors, walls, and woodwork to a sparkling gloss.

The much-loved Reverend Lorenzo Lyons, the missionary who had come from New England to the Islands in 1832, was now living and preaching to his flocks in Waimea. He was evangelical about the natives changing their ways, and the Hawaiians referred to him affectionately as *"Makua Laiana"*—*Makua* meaning Father, and *Laiana* being the counterpart of Lyons in the Hawaiian tongue. He was a tiny man but possessed a huge voice, and he preached and taught with true missionary fervor. Once big John Parker squeezed the little minister by way of greeting, and he later remarked, "I honestly thought there was nobody inside his clothes!"

Whenever it was practical or convenient, Parker invited the reverend to Mana to deliver a sermon. The reverend's wife taught school in Waimea, and when Parker's children were old enough, they were taken to Waimea, where Mrs. Lyons tutored them.

The two acres at Mana on the shoulder of Mauna Kea had to suffice until 1850, when a full section of 640 acres was granted John Parker's wife, Kipikane, by royal order befitting her *alii* rank. King Kamehameha III, of course, was the grantor. The files of the Hawaii State Archives have the transaction registered as Land Grant No. 358 to one John Palmer Parker.

The area ringed Parker's original two acres, obtained earlier from the king. All of the region was as it is today—breathtakingly beautiful, much of it highly satisfactory for grazing, and surrounded by forest lands extravagant with *maile, mamane,* and the brilliant yellow and red lehua trees.

Much hard work went into the building of Mana, and John proved himself to be a better than average craftsman. He gave Mana many of the architectural characteristics of his childhood home in New England. The making of furniture took much of his time, and he became very adept at it. With his native help, he continued building watersheds and constructing underground cisterns for holding rain water. He planted flowers and trees to soften and beautify the home. Mana was more than a little spiritually important to him. Even its name had an extra dimension, for it means "Motion and spirit that impels all thinking things and all objects of all thought." He knew that old Hawaiian legends stipulated that "Out of the concept of Mana the gods evolved."

Kipikane managed the household details, saw to the cooking of hearty meals for a hearty man and his family. Despite her manifold responsibilities, she had a reputation for always being immaculately dressed and adorned. She not only wore the best in tapa cloths, fashionably designed, but also often gowned herself in fine cambrics and muslins imported into the Islands. It was common for John to refer to her beauty and grace. But most of all, he praised her for her great talent and courage as a mother, and he counted her as the most complete person he had ever known.

Mana became their castle. They now had a home from where they could look across and beyond the valley, and up to the foot of the misty hills that folded peacefully into each other. For nearly twenty years Parker maintained Mana with a staff of retainers whom he clothed, housed, and fed. They were paid no coin of the realm, yet gladly accepted employment in caring for Parker's vast herd of cattle and sheep. They wanted for nothing in the way of larder for their tables. He was always the kind employer and the hospitable host. He was a devoutly ethical man, "good" in the Old Testament sense. With Kipikane's eager, unselfish help and cooperation, they lifted the homestead far out of the ordinary.

John Parker began to see many changes in the populace of the Island which he had come to call home; particularly since the missionaries had elected to give the Hawaiians a written language. The Hawaiians had had only a spoken language all these centuries, and their means of communication had thus been sorely handicapped. Now they were being taught to read and write. Their tongue only lent itself to seven consonants and the five vowels, but the mastery of the written word promised to be a tremendous boon to more communication and education.

Thanks to the efforts of the missionaries, printed books began showing up in the native language; and Parker applauded the step, thinking that someday the natives would actually be able to read the Bible! In fact, being such a godly man, interested in seeing the natives enlightened by Christianity, he took more and more interest in the work of the missionaries. This led to his developing a particular liking for the dedicated Reverend Lyons. Parker even became identified with the minister's church himself, the Congregational faith. Education, religious or otherwise, was on Parker's list of essential things, and he hired private teachers to tutor his children at home. He encouraged the printing of the wonderful Polynesian *meles* in book form so that the legends and history of the Islanders could be kept for posterity.

He was painstakingly careful in imparting his own knowledge to his children. He knew that a part of wisdom is to know the value of now, before it is gone forever. "Time is life," he used to tell them. "It's the only thing you can never get back." He also taught discipline so that the child would later understand the reason for obedience.

Another snippet of the early Parker life can be found in the late Emma Lyons Doyle's documentary, *Makua Laiana,* the story of her missionary grandfather who brought the Gospel to the Big Isle for a half century. She tells of how her grandparents horse-backed through the forest in the 1840s to the Parker Ranch and were dined and entertained there by the patriarch and his Hawaiian wife.

Reverend Lyons had had many trials, tribulations, and some successes during his years there as a practicing minister. He was loved and respected. John Parker was in the midst of blasting a cistern out of hard rock to obtain water for his herds of cattle and horses, but he was happy to drop all in order to welcome this man of cloth who was devoting his life to bettering the natives' situation. It was a close-knit family, with the Parker children eager to receive guests from off the ranch. Kipikane, proved to be the perfect hostess, despite her shyness and inability to speak a word of English. She set a table in "fine style." She served an elaborate dinner of imu-cooked chicken, fresh beef, sweet potatoes, *pa'i 'ai* (hard poi), and hard bread. Great fun was had by all, and when the Lyonses left, they departed with many gifts from the Parker larder.

In his diary, Reverend Lyons told of how they were offered all the peaches they could eat from the trees which had been growing on the Parker Ranch for five years. He described John Parker, Sr., as being a man with shaggy eyebrows, slow of speech, with little to say—and certainly a "good man." Praise of this kind from the Reverend Lyons was praise indeed, for the latter had, through years of self-sacrifice and all-out Christian work, endeared himself to the Hawaiians and had become one of the most outstanding and loved *haoles* on the Island.

In time, John Parker became so integrated with old Hawaiian ways that much of the time at Mana he was clad only in a *malo* (loin cloth). Studious and ever alert to learn, he became well versed in Hawaii's legends and history. He was able to deliver the land's *olis* (ancient chants) with a skill equal to that of many of the native chanters. He learned much from one aged native retainer at Mana. This retainer, the best chanter of the family, was Kipikane's own brother, Kapuaa. Kapuaa could mesmerize his audiences. He had an unusual vocal range which gave him the capacity for instantaneous transition from deep bass to high treble and back again. It was said that "he could sing duets with himself."

Kapuaa wore a very handsome horsehair belt, braided and knotted in different designs, with each knot representing the king, a chief, or his descendants. These he touched with graceful interpretations as he chanted the praises of the *aliis*. He was a comedian at heart and had the ability to inject humor into much of his work. When he elected to, he could hold a whole assembly in the palms of his hands, keeping them laughing all evening. The stories he told are still being told by the old people today.

In later years, hearing him chant at Mana, King Kalakaua asked Sam Parker to let Kapuaa live with him at Honolulu so that he could avail himself of the man's services. The king said he would clothe him, provide him with money, and, at the man's death, tend to his burial. Young Sam Parker referred Kalakaua to Uncle John Parker II, and the latter answered, "My Uncle Kapuaa remains in my home. I have sufficient to share with him."

However, at an even later date, Sam Parker took his chanting uncle to Honolulu to attend King Kalakaua's Jubilee festivities. Kapuaa was the leading chanter and created a sensation. The Hawaiians considered him a marvel, for the language of his chants was couched in deep *alii* words, and his gift of alternating from melodious bass to a sweet high tenor was spectacular. He resorted to clever monologues and was a master of interpretation, a ventriloquist who could swing from bass to tenor and down again. It was as though two separate persons were engaged in the chant, and his artistry probably could be compared with that of the fabled Polynesian chanters of *meles* and *olis*. Other celebrated chanters from Molokai, Maui, Oahu, and Kauai were present, but Kapuaa excelled them all, leaving the king and his guests entranced.

Kapuaa's genius thus had much to do with influencing John Parker I, encouraging him to chant his own stories about his own family—*haole* or otherwise. It was common for him to gather his own many guests around the fireside of his Mana home and, after Kapuaa had entertained at great length, Parker himself would, in turn, astonish everyone with his own exotic talent. He had the habit of galvanizing the attention of his company with anecdotes and stories of his experiences on the Big Island, in the Orient, at sea, and back on the mainland.

Still, as Hawaiianized as he became, John Parker remained thoroughly true to his old New England upbringing. His faith in Christianity was unshakable. Throughout the years he continued to summon his retainers around him to join in family prayers. Reverend Lyons had composed and translated many hymns which were sung at these gatherings, and often the diminutive minister with the booming voice himself took the lead in the worshiping and singing.

John Parker was already showing deep, personal interest in the the Parker Ranch men and their families, who were rapidly repaying him with faithful, loyal labor. "I'd walk the plank for them," he often said. When he was compelled to call upon them in extreme emergencies, they responded.

A charming description of Mana in 1851 can be found in a school composition written by Reverend Lyons' son, ten-year-old Albert. The minister had taken his family from Waimea to the Parker headquarters, and the youngster wrote:

"About eleven o'clock we got to the Parker place. Mr. Parker is a big man with shaggy eyebrows—not very talkative but he seemed glad to see us. His wife does not speak English, but she did everything she could to make us comfortable, and was very kind.

"There are several houses, some frame, some thatched, with lots of furniture and nice chairs, but the family likes to sit on the floor. They set the table for dinner, but Mrs. Parker would not sit with us; *'Hilahila,'* [I am ashamed] she said, but Mr. Parker, one of the sons, John, and his sister, Mary, sat with us. They had chicken cooked in an *imu,* fresh beef with sweet potatoes, *pia,* and hard bread. . . .

"There are ever so many peach trees planted on the place. They are only five years old, but they bear so many peaches that they have to be fed to the pigs. They are a bitter kind, but they smell ever so good. There are many flowers in the garden. They don't have to water anything because the fog comes over from Hamakua almost every evening and covers everything over with heavy dew.

"There are several big dogs that they use in driving cattle. They were wild dogs that were caught when they were puppies, and tamed. They would not come near us because we were strangers, and we children were afraid of them. They are very strong. One of them will hold a steer a year old without any trouble. We stayed at the Parker's until four o'clock, and then started home just as the fog began to come in."

The 1850s started out well for John: his first grandson, Samuel Parker, was born in 1853. The addition of this beautiful child to the family seemed to augur well for the balance of the fifties. Old John was supremely proud of his grandson. As for the patriarch's outlook on life by this time, he had the confidence of a man who had survived several landslides. He now took each day like a gift from God, no strings attached.

He had mellowed and had become more than a little philosophical. Although he had fought and elbowed his way through much of his thorny life, he had developed a credo: "You're here for only a little while. Don't hurry too fast, don't hurt anyone, and don't forget to stop and smell the flowers."

But happiness in the early Parker family had been tragically interrupted when Ebenezer died on March 22, 1855, at age twenty-six. Eben's death was a severe shock to everyone, and he was the first to be buried in Mana cemetery—a graveyard which today holds the remains of many people illustrious in Hawaiian history. Reverend Lyons read the funeral sermon. Then sorrow struck John Parker again five years later when his wife, Kipikane, died in 1860. She was laid to rest near their son Ebenezer at Mana. A deep, quiet loneliness now possessed old John.

About twelve months later a third major tragedy hit the old pioneer when Ebenezer's young widow, Kilia, was lost at sea, on February 16, 1861. That young woman's gravestone now also lay in the family cemetery at Kamuela—a lonely, fenced-in plot on the windy range.

Despite these calamitous blows, the old gentleman survived. He had always been willing to take great punishment, and he had stood up to it. By 1860 John Palmer Parker's herds had increased tremendously, and he was considered a wealthy man in his own right. Hard work, fair dealing, and intelligent planning had paid off handsomely. And life went on at the Parker domain. Another glimpse of old Parker Ranch life is found in C. de Varigny's *Fourteen Years in the Sandwich Islands*. It depicts the patriarchal system at Mana:

"Riding up the east coast [of Hawaii] and visiting Waipio, we at length came to Waimea, and at Manaaiole were the guests of John Parker. We were in the midst of patriarchal life. On our arrival, ten natives ran out to hold the bridles of our horses. Several young girls attracted by the noise, also came out. Some went to the dairy and the kitchen. The cattle were bellowing, the sheep bleating, and a sweet odor of dinner greeted our olfactory nerves. We were lodged in a box or, if you like it better, in a house of compartments all of varnished koa—a wood of the country which looks like mahogany. Roof, doors, partitions, ceilings, floors, the interior as well as the exterior, all made of koa; all very like one might say a gigantic toy.

"Mr. Parker often spoke of Kamehameha I. We spent the evening with him and he had a peculiar charm as a narrator. I have spent few evenings so agreeable."

On September 12, 1864, John Parker gave a summation of his life in a letter written at Hamakua, Hawaii. It gives us an insight to his character and personality in the Indian summer of his life. He was partially blind and failing rapidly by this time. It reads:

"I have been living on this island forty-eight years. I sailed from the Sandwich Islands in a ship belonging to Davis and Winship for Canton, China, and arrived there safe with a cargo of sandalwood.

"It being war time with England and America [War of 1812], we were blockaded two years in China. I was tired of stopping there and left for the Sandwich Islands, but did not arrive until 16 months after. The vessel that I sailed in went to the Columbia River and California before going to the Islands, but I have never been away from the Islands since.

"I have had but one wife and she has been dead four years. I have but one son living [John] and he is a good son and a great blessing to me.

"I went ashore at Hawaii under the protection of Kamehameha I, and have lived to see five kings. The Sandwich Islands have been greatly improved by our American countrymen, by many sugar plantations and other improvements.

"I have a great grazing farm of many thousand acres; and a great many bullocks, horses, sheep, hogs, etc. That is my business, the raising of stock. I am very comfortable, thank God. I do not use strong drinks, and that is all that keeps people from being in good circumstances. Rum is the curse of this country. Many a good trader is ruined by rum."

At the age of seventy-seven, in 1867, John Palmer Parker's health had deteriorated even further. His weathered face, and hair the texture and color of iron filings, showed it. He was dying—and those around him knew it. He had lived hard and fully.

Parker had a keen sense of humor, and when some loved ones alluded to his now advanced age, he laughed softly, saying "Death is an incurable disease that men and women are born with; it gets them sooner or later." There was merriment in his voice even while he was failing noticeably.

One day, when he sensed he would soon die, he sent for his missionary friends, the Congregationalist ministers Reverend Lorenzo Lyons and Reverend Elias Bond. They came to Mana at his bidding, and Parker indicated that he needed something now tantamount to the last rites.

The ministers talked to him, heard his wishes, and granted them. He was duly received into their church. Parker knew he was no candidate for sainthood, but he was trying to be the Christian he wanted to be. Communion was served to him, as well as to some church members who had come in.

Parker died a few months later on March 25, 1868, at Honolulu. He died with a calm and tranquil look on his face.

His body was prepared for shipment back to Hawaii for burial. Shortly later, Lyons made a note in his running log: "Journal, April 9, 1868. The steamer brought the remains of Mr. J. P. Parker. They passed in Mr. Spencer's mule wagon, with a large company on horses. . . . Sat. 11. All Waimea gone to attend Mr. Parker's funeral. I am unable to go. . . . 18th. John Parker II called yesterday to see about the will, I being a witness."

The old patrician was laid to rest at the side of his beloved Kipikane who had preceded him by eight years. Leis were heaped high, marguerites, maile, and the brilliant cerise *akulikuli*.

The Parkers' graves are still on the slopes of Mauna Kea, where the wind drives the mists, where the ironwoods wave their branches like the flowing robes of old *kahunas*. The little graveyard is a silent place. Only the winds, rains, and sunshafts now play on the tombstone of the young sailor who jumped ship on the Kona Coast to seek his lot with a people who learned to love him.

Parker had disposed of his possessions in a loosely drawn will. Mary Low's detailed letter to Richard Smart, dated January 25, 1932, reads in part:

"In the latter's [John Palmer Parker, Sr.] will he left to his grandson, Sam Parker, the share of what he would have given of his estate to his son, Ebenezer, one half of all his lands, sheep, bullock, horses, etc; also what cash he had on hand at the time of his death; also the original koa dwelling known as Mana Hale [house] and joint privileges with two tanks, dairy, and servants' quarters on the upper part of the Mana seven acres home lot.

"J. P. Parker II to be the guardian of Sam Parker till of age, then give him what is willed to him. But it was J. P. Parker I's wish that J. P. Parker II's grazing land and stock and Sam Parker's grazing land and stock, should remain together if possible for them to agree. From the old Mana house, mentioned above, to the lower part of the Mana seven acre home lot, all houses belonged to John P. Parker II; also one half of all his lands, sheep, bullock, horses, etc. and cash.

"He also left to Sam, Mary and Nancy, the three children of Ebenezer on their coming of age, to each one, one thousand dollars, and to Mary two pieces of land in Kohala to be hers upon his death. His granddaughter Nancy got no land.

"To the children of his only daughter, Mary Ann Fuller Waipa, who died nine years before John P. Parker I, he remembered only two of her daughters—his grandchildren; leaving to Martha Fuller Low upon his death, two pieces of land in Kohala, and to Ann Waipa [who later became the mother of Purdy] two pieces of land—one in Kohala, one in Paako, Hamakua."

Mary Low added more details of the will in a later letter:

"I omitted some items in describing Mana to you and how John P. Parker I left the buildings on this seven acre homestead —the seven acres being a part of the 640 acres of land mentioned in his will as the land surveyed by T. Metcalf. J. P. Parker I's will mentions in part as follows: 'One half of all lands, etc.—one half of 640 acres of land surveyed by T. Metcalf with all improvements thereon to J. P. Parker II, excepting part of the dwelling house lot and old house as I will mention hereafter; all chests, trunks and clothing, guns, pistols, powders, lead, yokes, chains, and all other things that belong to the premises.

" 'J. P. Parker II is to give Samuel Parker the old dwelling house known as Mana Hale and joint privilege with the two tanks on the upper part of the house lot and the dairy house and the house that the natives live in—with four rooms from the old dwelling house to the lower part of the lot all houses belong to J. P. Parker II.' "

The old "hospitable prince of the mountain" left a great deal of material wealth to his beneficiaries. Yet, in reality, he left another and even greater legacy to them which went wholly unmentioned—and that was the legacy found in the name of Parker itself.

Of John Parker's grandchildren, the second-born of Ebenezer and Kilia was named Mary Ann Kaulalani Parker II, named after her aunt. Her grandfather sent her to the Convent of the Sacred Heart at Honolulu, where she became a top scholar and a model of excellent behavior.

By 1868 a steady and substantial young Englishman, James Woods, asked for Mary Ann's hand in marriage. Woods was currently working for the firm of Janion & Green in Waimea, and John Parker knew him well. Feeling that it would be a good marriage, Parker sent word to his granddaughter and the nuns at the convent.

Mary Ann believed in the old gentleman and wanted to please him. Quietly and reasonably, she discussed the possible marriage with her grandfather, and her answer was that she would marry James Woods. Mary Ann obediently married James Woods at her grandfather's bedside. She, of course, was still very young and hardly knew the gentleman whom she was marrying, but her grandfather had said, "I will die happier knowing that you will be the wife of a good and upright man."

Mary Ann and James Woods were blessed with eight children. In later years, upon Woods's death, Mary took a second husband, Charles K. Stillman. By this marriage she had one son, Charles K. Stillman, Jr. Her grandfather had left her in his will the Waiapuka home which he first lived in after King Kamehameha I had died. After her own death in Honolulu, Mary Ann was buried in the Kohala Catholic graveyard on the Big Island. The property went to her children, except one-half acre, which was deeded to the Catholic Mission for a church. The church was built, and the legendary Father Damien was its pastor before he became the martyr priest of the leper settlement on the Island of Molokai.

In 1860 Eben's son, Christian, died at the age of ten. Nancy Parker, Eben's daughter, lived on seemingly not involved with the history of the ranch.

Samuel K. Parker, son of Ebenezer and Kilia Parker, was not quite three years old when his father died. His grandparents immediately took charge of him. He was eight years old when his mother drowned at sea. At an early age he was sent to the Catholic school at Ahuimanu in the district of Koolau, Oahu, spending all of his vacations at Mana on the Big Isle. Later, when he attended the very select and private Punahou School in Honolulu, he continued spending his vacations at Mana. When his grandfather, died in 1868, Samuel was fourteen years old.

Samuel's living routine continued the same, whether in school on Oahu or living at Mana with his Uncle J. P. Parker II and Aunt Hanai Parker. He was idolized by them, given his own way, and everything he desired. Although Hanai became even more frugal as she grew older, she continued to give him all the cash that he wanted.

On the ranch, Samuel was treated as a crown prince. He had inherited the handsome appearance of his father, Ebenezer, and certainly all of the grace and charm of his mother, Kilia. In Waimea as a teen-ager, he cut as fine a figure as his father had before him. It was common to see him in Waimea town riding a prancing white horse and dressed in a stunning white riding outfit.

8

Calamitous Days

A FTER John Palmer Parker's death in 1868, real disintegration began to set in at the vast Parker holdings. John Parker II made efforts, but little or nothing was done to improve the stock or stimulate the management.

Much of the huge ranch region was still unfenced, as the vast herds increased. Cattle roamed almost unreachable regions and again turned wild and lean. They were to be found hidden in the forests of ohia, koa, and *wili-wili*, penetrating the tangles of cactus and *kiawe* of the local lands. For a while the profitable thrust which John Parker I had given the ranch kept it on a paying basis, but the magic hand of the original founder was sorely missing, and the dry rot of time was beginning to set in.

Young Samuel, in Honolulu, was still the dandy, and his flamboyance was netting him an incredible reputation. He boasted, "I try everything in life except incest and folk dancing," and was often seen with Harriet Panana Napela, a beautiful girl from Maui. She was descended directly from one of the ancient Maui kings on her paternal side. Her mother was the former Kitty Richardson of Honolulu, daughter of a wealthy and important *haole* family. Her second name of Panana, meaning "a compass," had been given to one of her ancestors by the king of Maui as a compliment to her rare beauty, which as the monarch said, "steered everyone to her."

Mary E. Low, one of her antecedents, once wrote of her to Richard Smart: "Panana was certainly a beauty! Even in her maturity she was one of the most perfect types of Hawaiian beauty and was admired as much abroad where she was well known. She was brought up very carefully in her youth, her father placing her in charge of the missionaries at the Maunaolu Seminary at Makawao, Maui. She dressed in tight dresses— meaning she did not wear *holokus*—and always rode back and forth from the Seminary to her home in Wailuku sidesaddle; and she never went without corsets, so that she had a very small waist.

"Everything in her home was of the best—a two-story house with fine furniture. She was raised as an *alii* [chieftess], her uncle being a very rich chief, leaving her all his fortune upon his death. He was a distinguished imperial-looking chief with a straight profile and would have stood as a fine model for a bronze statue. He used, as the old Maui chiefs did when talking, the *t* for *k*."

The young couple had a love affair, and as prospective parents, they wished to marry, and Sam was candid about it with Panana's parents. Mr. Napela naturally was shocked, but he was willing to go along with the wedding. However, Mrs. Napela was aghast and would not countenance such a tie. She sent Sam away and kept her daughter at home, where the baby was born out of wedlock.

In addition, through subterfuge, Mrs. Napela convinced the naive Panana that the baby had died at birth. In reality, the angered mother of Panana had sent the infant away with a woman relative who raised the child in secret for five years, eventually putting it in an orphanage to be raised by nuns.

It was an episode of crushing grief for the young unwed mother. Sam, too, was heavy with sorrow. A word from him would have given Panana hope, but Mrs. Napela had cut off all means of communication between the two lovers. For Panana there was nothing left that mattered. She was almost destroyed.

Sam continued living at Punahou, trying to drown his sorrow in forgetfulness and studies, deceiving himself that time would take care of everything and that he and Panana would someday be reunited. But, after many weeks of no word from her, Sam began to doubt. His grades fell off at school, and even Aunt Hanai took him to task.

Sam finally went to the Napela home again and sought to be admitted. This time he would not be deterred and insisted that he be given Panana's hand in marriage. Between failing health and heartbreak over the loss of her baby, Panana was in a sorrowful state. Sam's return was a reunion that took all the anguish out of separation. Happily for the young couple, Mrs. Napela had finally reconciled herself to the situation and gave her consent to the marriage. The vibrant Sam Parker charm had ultimately won out. Panana's uncle, Kuiheiani, a very high chief, gave them a fabulous wedding.

The marriage took place in Honolulu in 1871 and was attended by all the Parkers as well as most of the high society of the Islands. The papers made much of the event, and it launched Sam and Panana into a new social world which outshone anything they had ever experienced.

Pomp and ceremony attended the arrival of the newlyweds at Mana. John P. Parker II built a new koa cottage for them next to the Mana wing which Ebenezer and Kilia had originally occupied. The cottage still stands. It was called "Waialeale"— the name of Panana's maiden home in Maui. When Sam and Panana arrived at Kawaihae, a prancing horse was brought down for the bride, which she rode sidesaddle. Her manner of riding so surprised the Waimea natives that they likened her curvaceous figure to that of a champagne glass on a horse.

The newlyweds were welcomed deliriously in Waimea, despite the fact that the bride, with her *alii* ways, did not care much for Aunt Hanai. However, with Sam's and Panana's taste for entertaining and good living, they were soon the center of all social activities. They did much to improve Mana itself by beautifying the gardens and structures. Partying gaily, arranging hunting trips—Sam was a skilled marksman—picnicking and general entertaining, they demonstrated that they were more than a little willing to share their riches with everybody. They became the hub of society in the entire region.

Mary E. Low writes of these times: "As we came home out of school we spent many days out with the cowboys, after cattle, or camping up the mountain, feasting on pigs and other game. We were all young, and life at Mana in Sam and Panana's time was one round of joy with everybody happy."

In fact, the Parker-Napela marriage catapulted Sam and his wife into a merry-go-round world of parties and events rivaling those of the monarch of all the Islands, King Kalakaua. The king and his queen Kapiolani at Iolani Palace on Oahu were attempting to revive the sparkling culture of Hawaii which had been lost for so long. Sam Parker and Panana continued to revel in lavish parties and the grandeur of rich, formal occasions. The friendship and understanding of this privileged foursome continued to flourish. Throughout Kalakaua's life, he entertained politicians, upper-echelon military men, industrialists, artists, and celebrities from all over the world.

With Sam Parker's financial and social position in the Islands, it is no wonder that the king dubbed him "Colonel," and delegated him as a lifetime member of the House of Nobles. The Parkers were entertained royally at the palace on occasion after occasion.

But back at Mana on the Big Isle Samuel Parker never let the world forget that he had his own dynasty there. The ranch's reputation for high living was fabled. Mounted guests, carriage trade, people on all manner of horse- and bullock-drawn vehicles often clogged the narrow dirt road leading up to Mana from the lower levels. Mana itself was enlarged, beautified, the grounds enlarged and elaborately landscaped. The salons and accommodations for visitors were as majestic as those of a courtly domain. Edwardian elegance, imported furnishings, damask-draped walls, musicians and entertainers, food and drink to suit the taste of the most discriminating of epicures—all contributed to the reputation of the new order of Parkers.

Sam spent more and more time at the palace and was spoken of as "the handsomest man at court." As one who believed in mutual exchange, the "Lord of Mana" entertained and housed influential people on a grand scale.

But these were the very avenues which brought the Parker Ranch down to a sorry state, financially and administratively. Everything had become secondary to the social whirl. Colonel Sam Parker grew older and gave most of his attention to hosting and being hosted; he spent with a free hand, and began to dissipate the fortune amassed by three generations of Parkers.

The Samuel Parkers had nine children. Panana accompanied her two daughters, Helen and Eva, to a finishing school in London. While the mother and daughters were there, Sam learned that the supposedly "dead" baby born out of wedlock to them some years before was actually in a convent in Honolulu being raised by nuns. It was Mary Parker Woods, Sam's sister, who had somehow learned the secret and passed it along to her brother. Astonished that the child was actually alive, Sam began visiting her at the convent. Mary was her baptized name, and Sam idolized her from his first visit at the convent.

Sam wrote Panana in Europe and told her of his plans to bring Mary home. Surprisingly, Panana felt that the young girl should remain in the custody of the church. Possibly fear of scandal influenced her. But Sam Parker was adamant and arranged for the child to be brought home.

Mary Low wrote of the girl: "Her full name was Mary Kihalani Parker. She had a very timid nature, gentle mannered, and was small, so different from the rest of her brothers and sisters—all big people. My heart went out to the girl from the first.

"When her mother, Panana, returned home, she made the best of everything and the girl remained in the home of the parents until her marriage to Charles Maguire, when she lived at Kahua Ranch which was then owned by Charles Maguire's father."

During the late 1870s and on into the 1880s and 1890s, the ranch was occupied and "operated" jointly by John Palmer Parker II and his nephew, Samuel Parker. The word *operated* is used advisedly here, for the cattle kingdom's operation was now a far cry in efficiency from that of the late John Parker I. Under the new joint supervision, the ranch still had beauty and charm, but the old successful concentration on the cattle business itself was in steep decline.

Mary Low writes of those days:

"John P. Parker II, having no children, adopted the oldest son of Sam Parker, his nephew who was named after him—John Palmer Parker III. This child lived with his grand uncle, J. P. Parker II, and Hanai Parker, as their own son. Prior to the buying of Puuopelu, the Parkers had a stopping place in Waimea known as Waiemi; not much of a house on it, but as I remember it, the large center room was frequently partitioned off with calico curtains to form rooms for family and guests. It was a stopping place when going from Mana to Kawaihae, or from Kawaihae to Mana.

"J. P. Parker II or Sam Parker used it often during drives or shipping times of cattle, etc. The grounds were quite a forest that I gloried in, for peaches, figs, bananas and oranges were abundant there. The Parkers also had a house at Kawaihae; not much to look at but thoroughly used and enjoyed by the Parker family. No one cared to sleep in its two bedrooms for they were haunted. Only the *lanai* and kitchen were used. Everybody sleeping on mattresses or mats under the cocoanut trees, with mosquito nets strung across from tree to tree.

"This place was very frequently used especially during the *aku* and *akule* fish season, for Sam was a great fisherman and had his boat houses on the beach where he kept canoes and double fishing canoes; also his boats. One boat was named *Kahilu.* Kawaihae was rather active in those days with many expert

Hawaiian fishermen living there. When leaving or returning from ships at Kawaihae, the Parkers and their guests never landed at the wharf, but their own boats, manned by a Hawaiian crew called for them from ship to beach opposite their house at Kawaihae. We were carried off canoe or boat on the natives' backs to the beach.

"Sam Parker, during his youth when not at school, lived altogether with his Uncle and Aunt Hanai at Mana. In John P. Parker II's time, living was very primitive in those days and mostly Hawaiian was spoken. The forest surroundings were beautiful! Where the schoolhouse now is there was a horse pen, and nearby was the storehouse for saddles, harness, etc. and ox carts house. Also a house for salting hides nearby, and a meat house, all in sight of the Mana house and the Kapuaikai house.

"In Sam and Panana's time this was all quickly changed; these stone houses were torn down and rebuilt out of sight, the horse pen also moved out of sight, and lawns and a garden built up. In no time the garden was certainly beautiful for everything grew rank in those days; ginger grew wild. Leis made out of their buds in many styles were marvels.

"The family used the Waialeale cottage built for Sam and Panana as a guest cottage, using the larger Mana *hale* which had more comfort. Panana's wedding gifts of silver were many, and she always had good service and stewards in her many homes. It naturally grew to be a custom always to dress for dinner for company and to come to dinner with flowers in the hair, or a lei or corsage bouquet. Some marvelous leis were made out of flowers grown on the place.

"After Eva and Helen were born, Sam Parker added a wing to the Kapuaihali cottage built for J. P. Parker II and Hanai. This wing was of ordinary lumber painted with corrugated iron roofing and consisted of a bathroom, a dining room, kitchen and pantries and bedrooms with closets and verandahs which were occupied by Sam and Panana and their children. It was named Eva Hale after their daughter Eva. The whole connected buildings formed the letter *E*. Mana was always primitive with *hales* [toilets] outside, and bathhouse outside, and kerosene lamps.

"This whole place at Puuopelu had been planted by the Notleys who sold it to John P. Parker II. Notley was an Englishman raising sheep, selling out to go into cane at Paauilo. He married a Hawaiian woman by the name of Kaluahine. She was a niece of Kipikane Rachael Parker, her brother's daughter. Aunt Hanai was never much about having a garden, cared little for trees and shrubs, and was always thinning the place out till it got barren.

" . . . J. P. Parker III lived mostly at Puuopelu. There was a big lake of water below this Puuopelu lot where fruit trees, especially figs and peaches grew, where Johnnie . . . had a boat and played in the lake daily. It was cold water and Waimea is always cold. When people warned Aunt Hanai not to allow the boy to play so much in such cold water and weather, she'd answer: 'It is one way of growing strong.' He was born a strapping boy, and I do think that the inflammatory rheumatism that he got later on was his finish and that the cause of it began with the boat and lake at Waimea.

"The course of the water that plowed into this lake was turned away later during, I think, Paul Jarrett's management of the Parker Ranch. Uncle John built a two-story house at Puuopelu for Sam and his family. The Sam Parker family went down there frequently for days and weeks, at times just for the day, or to have breakfast or lunch on the way to or from Mana to Kawaihae. The Sam Parker family used Mana altogether, though Uncle John and Hanai, when they went to Mana, used their private upstairs room in Kapuaihali."

In the mid-1890s, events led to further changes in ranch ownership. Elizabeth Jane Lanakila Dowsett Parker became a major factor in property title switches shortly after she married John Parker III, the son of Sam Parker. She was to prove to be a stalwart character, an extraordinary woman whom everyone loved as "Aunt Tootsie."

Aunt Tootsie came by her intrepid spirit naturally, for she was the great-granddaughter of Captain Samuel James Dowsett, a British naval officer who settled in Honolulu in 1828. The Dowsett men were all entrepreneurs and men of quality and vision. James I. Dowsett, the grandson of Captain Dowsett, was Tootsie's father. He was known to the Hawaiians as Kimo Pelekane—"British Jim"—and he was loved by them. Other than children of missionary parents, James I. Dowsett was reputed to be the first Caucasian born in the then Sandwich Islands. Tootsie came by her beauty from a long line of handsome men and women.

Born in the year 1872, her world was one of wealth and position from the start. But it never altered the down-to-earth qualities which so endeared her to her friends and loved ones. Her mother and father were founders of the Honolulu Maternity Hospital.

The Parkers and the Dowsetts had social ties dating far back. James Dowsett was one of the wealthiest men in the Islands, some of his fortune based on ranching in the Schofield Barracks region of Oahu. His other interests, too, were on a large scale —including lumber schooners and whaling ships. He doted on his family and spared nothing in giving his daughters happiness. He sent Tootsie to Springfield, Massachusetts, to attend finishing school, and, after she found New England too cold, he transferred her to Mills College in San Francisco, where she became a social leader renowned for her good and charitable deeds.

When she wasn't reigning as a much-loved queen in San Francisco, she was doing likewise at Puuopelu on Hawaii. She had developed into a highly intelligent and beautiful woman.

Tootsie first met John Parker III at a dance at the royal palace. The hostess Queen Liliuokalani, made sure that the two would meet. The two young people were married a few months later. Their marriage took place at the Dowsett family home in Honolulu in 1893. Tootsie was stunningly gowned and jeweled, and wrote later in her diary that her wedding dress was made of many yards of Brussels lace over ivory satin, with a train six feet long entirely embroidered with seed pearls.

But their happiness dissolved before a full year had elapsed. In 1893 in Honolulu, John Parker III, only a nineteen-year-old newlywed, was struck down with a fatal illness, while his young wife, Tootsie, was also bedridden, in the throes of a difficult and painful childbirth.

The girl bride had full knowledge of the condition of her young husband. Her spasms of agonizing pain worsened and, fearful that John would suffer more by hearing her tormented cries, she heroically jammed a towel between her jaws and remained silent throughout her anguish. Tiny Annie Thelma Parker was born during all this travail.

On March 8, 1894—just a few months later—John Parker III died. It was naturally a stunning blow to the young mother, and she was numbed by the loss. But she carried on and took her baby to Mana, where she stayed with her father-in-law, John Parker II and his wife Hanai. The newborn child was given the Hawaiian name of Kahiluonapuaapiilani—"The fair one of the clan or family group of Piilani"—and she was all that the name implied. Tootsie kept her at the ranch until she was five years old, and then they moved back to San Francisco.

Ebenezer Parker was supposed to be the "swinger" of the family, but Samuel Parker, the son of Ebenezer and Kilia, was to outdo him. Whether he was spending his time in Kamuela on Hawaii or at Punahou School on Oahu, he was a dashing young man with the ladies. In adult life he was a ducal sort of man. He had a crisp, stamped kind of smile, made friends easily, but when crossed could become vindictive. When entertaining, he was fastidious in his manner of dress. But when hunting or fishing, he took on the appearance of an unfrocked bartender.

He introduced new *alii* blood into the Parker family when he married the beautiful Harriet Panana Napela, a direct descendant of that great Maui king, Kekaulike. A feather cape which had belonged in her family from the time of Kekaulike is still in the Bishop Museum at Honolulu today and it is known as the Parker cape.

A new Mana to serve as the family mansion was built by Samuel Parker. It was constructed on a site about seven miles from Kamuela, just beyond the district of Hamakua. The structure itself is gone now; all but several stone steps, a portion of the formal garden, and a few trees still mark its spot. Beautiful *Ka ui o Mana* (Beauty of Mana) blooms there now, and it is said that it is the same plant which graced the homestead in the old days.

Archives reveal that the place had a splendor unknown to Hawaii in the past. The library is described as "Worthy of the royal trains that swept the floor." At formal dinner parties scores of candles shone on European crystal. The ceiling in that second Mana was curved and set with ribs of koa—shining, hand-wrought work on which no expense was spared.

A miniature replica of this second Mana is preserved under a glass case in the museum which Richard Smart has instituted at the first Mana. Built to scale, it shows the many-memoried features of the old sloping-roofed home with its koa walls. The koa wood in the museum was hewn and hauled from the high forests of Waimea; much of it was salvaged from the demolished second Mana house.

Sam Parker not only perpetuated the hospitality which his grandfather, the old patriarch, had begun at Mana, but he also enlarged upon it, spending, freely with no care for the future, living the life of a child playing in a well-filled sandbox. Mana became the stopping place for all royal tours of the Big Island, in addition to offering hospitable harbor to an endless influx of travelers, explorers, state dignitaries, missionaries, military officers, and just plain friends.

Sam Parker and Panana also maintained a large home in Honolulu—a long white bungalow on the *mauka* (mountain) side of King Street. There were guest cottages, servants' quarters, and stables noted for fine horses. The elaborate establishment was one of King Kalakaua's favorite visiting spots.

Sam Parker spent much time at the court of King Kalakaua, who was also a man of great charisma. A knowledgeable confidant of the King, Sam carried himself handsomely like a true *alii*. It was said that he appeared so omnipotent that he could get by without God.

In time, Sam became a nobleman under King Kalakaua. The two men had much in common. Both were lovers of gaudy, ostentatious parties, expensive cuisine, and merrymaking. Both doted on hunting and gambling at cards—to say nothing of drinking. Both loved money, and Sam himself used to quip, "The only thing that money can't buy is poverty."

Both were descended from highborn Hawaiians. Kalakaua was a direct descendant of Kameeiamoku and Keaweaheulu, distinguished counselors of Kamehameha the Great. With Sam being a great-great-grandchild of King Kamehameha I, it was natural that Sam and Kalakaua had an additional feeling of empathy for one another. They fraternized and socialized together, the two of them even making several trips to San Francisco. This was all simple for the king, but for Sam it meant huge spending which the ranch could ill afford.

Through more and more neglect and lack of foresight, the ranch disintegrated even further. This did not keep Sam Parker from continuing to live like a maharajah, although his income lessened appreciably.

In November 1890 the King went on an ill-fated trip to California and was taken seriously ill. He died there on January 20, 1891. But Sam's advice and support still remained at a premium at the royal court, for Kalakaua's brilliant sister, Queen Liliuokalani, began her reign on January 29, 1891, and made Sam a member of her cabinet. He became one of the two cabinet officers who stood by her when she proclaimed her new constitution. The other members of the cabinet refused to sign the document, and leading citizens were appealed to for support and advice.

After a long debate with the cabinet, the queen yielded to some degree and announced to the assemblage that the proclamation would be postponed for a short time. There were many meetings, and finally steps were taken for the formation of a provisional government. There were additional mass meetings, more cabinet sessions, and on January 16, 1893, the U.S.S. *Boston* landed a force of armed men to protect American interests. The presence of American troops in the city made possible a bloodless revolution.

Two companies of volunteer troops were placed on duty in the palace grounds, and the queen, upon advice of Sam Parker and other ministers, surrendered her authority under protest. Sam's name is on the abdication which the queen signed "under duress" when the revolutionary group took over on January 17, 1893.

Queen Liliuokalani reigned less than two years, and her attempts at governing had been as turbulent as had her brother's. Sam Parker had remained a solid loyalist all through her troubles. Even when she demanded the resignation of all cabinet members who were not in accord with her, he still stuck by her. It was during this period that the chains of circumstance were forged which led to the abolition of the Hawaiian monarchy and annexation of the whole Hawaiian archipelago by the United States.

In his capacity as a member of the royal cabinet, Sam had been highly thought of; even the *haoles* and those outside the court had great regard for his administrative talents. One newspaper of the day printed: "Col. Sam Parker is the only member of the cabinet through whose veins flows the native Hawaiian blood, and he is beyond question one of the most prominent and popular Hawaiians in the monarchy."

In fact, important spokesmen of the day insisted that Sam Parker was the only member of Queen Liliuokalani's cabinet for whom the Revolutionists had a feeling of warmth. His advice and suggestions were sought until 1898, when the United States annexed the Islands. Sam might well have gone on to bigger and more important levels in the royal court had not the monarchy been dissolved.

Being a long-time member of King Kalakaua's Privy Council had its glamour for Sam, but while he was hobnobbing with the monarch and other social and royal figures, the Parker Ranch was being sorely neglected.

Its income fell off dramatically, and it is no wonder then that Sam Parker fell victim to advice that he should go in for sugarcane raising in lieu of cattle raising. Claus Spreckles, the California sugar magnate, approached him with a plan to convert Parker Ranch into a sugar plantation. Spreckles had already made millions with his own sugar ventures on Maui and in the Phillipines, and he convinced Sam that their combined efforts with the Parker Ranch acreage would net tremendous profits.

Spreckles' proposition sounded like a life-saving expedient to Sam, who realized that many of the ranch's facets were undeveloped. The herds consisted of about 5,000 head of wild cattle, and, as the result of inbreeding and inattention, they were too scraggly for top marketability.

Claus Spreckles convinced Sam that turning the lower half of the Paauhau lands into a sugar plantation would net large profits. This would be just for "starters." He even promised to advance Sam the money to build the mill and start it going under able men while Sam planted the cane. By the time the mill was erected, the cane would be ready for grinding. Sam immediately put the sugar proposition up to his uncle, John Parker II. The latter frowned upon the idea at once and told Sam not to go into any cane planting as they knew nothing about the business. "Stick to what we already know—cattle and stock raising," Uncle John insisted. "It brings us sufficient to live on for the whole family. Why go into something that might fail?"

But Sam was stubborn and totally sold on Spreckles' advice. His mind was closed. He went ahead and planted great acreage of cane, which just about broke Uncle John's heart. In fact, the old gentleman worried so much about the prospects of the sugarcane planting that he began concealing cattle profits—such as they were—in various places in case of need. He obviously feared bankruptcy would result from the sugarcane project.

But none of his uncle's fears daunted Sam, who remained sold on Spreckles' plan. Sam and John II were totally different in their thinking. Sam persisted in the cane planting, continued his lavish spending, and soon had the ranch running deeply into debt. The new project began to fail early. By the time the cane crop was ripe and ready for grinding, the mill was not completed, and a costly loss of time ensued while Sam had to hold his big crop until after the regular Paauilo and Honokaa crops were ground. Too late, he realized that the whole sugar-cane idea had been built on quicksand and that it was leading to financial disaster for the ranch. Sam went heavily in debt to Spreckles, and even Sam was later to admit, "The whole thing was a roller coaster ride conceived in chaos and executed in panic."

In fact, this error on the part of Sam had much to do with his uncle continuing to worry and fret over the ranch's shrinking income. Everything became a crisis with the older man. Things were so bad that a sad forgetfulness took hold of Uncle John's mind, and he couldn't remember where he had secreted the monies. He'd try to recall, but to no avail. To this day some of the hidden funds have never been found.

John P. Parker II's condition grew progressivley worse, and Sam Parker got the head *luna* (manager), Paul Jarrett, from the Paauhau Plantation, to manage the Parker Ranch. Jarrett plugged up many of the holes in the cattle kingdom's weakened structure, but Uncle John's mind continued to deteriorate. He was in a fog of confusion, and everyone on the ranch did everything possible to help him. Mary Parker Woods Stillman, his niece, nursed him in a dedicated way, taking him to such places as Kawaihae, Honolulu, and California for rest and treatment. In desperation, Hanai Parker even had him treated by Maui *kahunas.*

But it was all to no avail. John Parker II now walked with a shuffling gait, his shoulders stooped, his hands thrust into his trouser pockets.

He died in Honolulu at Sam's home on November 22, 1891. Great tribute and homage was paid to the old gentleman. As he was a life member of the House of Nobles during the reign of King David Kalakaua and also a member of the Privy Council, the government flags flew at half-mast out of respect for the deceased.

The funeral services, held at Sam's home in Honolulu, were on a magnificent scale, with great banks of flowers and the impressive Royal Hawaiian Band playing solemn music appropriate to the loss of so important a member of society. Every dignitary, royalist, statesman, politician, and person of importance who could possibly attend the funeral was present, including Queen Liliuokalani, Governor Cleghorn, the princes Kawananakoa and Kalanianaole, Chamberlain Robertson, Chief Justice Judd, and all the foreign commissioners who were members of the Privy Council. John Parker II's relatives and personal friends, were there en masse, deeply bereaved.

John Parker II's remains were taken on the steamer *Kinau* to Kawaihae for burial at Mana. His was one more body laid to rest in the family cemetery.

Shortly after this, the Parker family suffered another loss. Young John Palmer Parker III died in Honolulu at his father's house on March 8, 1894. He died the age of only nineteen years, two months, and two days. His funeral services, too, were held at the Sam Parker home in Honolulu, and the body was removed to Mana for burial. Having not attained his majority, J. P. Parker III had not inherited his uncle's estate. Instead, it went directly to his baby daughter, Annie Thelma Parker.

The reason for the inheritance might seem a little vague without some explanation. John Parker II had adopted his grandnephew (Sam Parker's son), John III, who automatically became John Parker II's natural heir. Then, with John Parker III still a minor at the time of his death, in addition to the fact that he had made no will, one-third of the inheritance would, under ordinary circumstances, go to his widow, Elizabeth Dowsett Parker (Tootsie), and two-thirds to the child. Tootsie, however, had relinquished her dower right in favor of little Thelma. Consequently, in 1894 the little girl came into full ownership of her father's half-share of the estate.

9

Alfred Wellington Carter

I T IS OBVIOUS that sheer desperation on Sam Parker's part had driven him into the negotiations with Spreckles on the sugarcane deal, which had resulted in such depletion of the ranch's financial status. But now a new and shining element was about to bless the Parker Ranch: a man named Alfred Wellington Carter.

Elizabeth "Tootsie" Parker, now the widow of John Parker III, was in Honolulu in September 1899 to ask Mr. Carter to become legal guardian of her fatherless daughter, Thelma. Thelma was but five years old at the time. This, of course, also involved the guardianship and management of the child's half of the Parker Ranch property. There were troubles, Tootsie admitted honestly to Carter.

One day Samuel Parker, now owning the other half of the ranch, came into Carter's office. He offered his interest to be managed and controlled—provided that the Carter would accept the guardianship which Tootsie had suggested. This offer seemed simple enough, but it was fraught with more than one secret and complex problem.

Carter was a big man with a gentle smile. His voice had the timbre of sincerity and friendliness, and he had a no nonsense, decisive manner. He hesitated only a moment, then said emphatically, "It's a deal." Thus Carter was appointed guardian of the property of Thelma Parker on September 25, 1899.

He immediately started concluding his own business affairs in Honolulu. But within a few months, in January 1900, an epidemic of bubonic plague broke out in Honolulu's China-town. As an emergency measure, Carter was put in charge of the guards and transportation in the Chinatown district. Under the auspices of the local fire department, a condemned area of build-ings was put to the torch to prevent widespread contamination. The tinder-dry structures sucked in the flames like prairie grass, and the conflagration got out of control when pushed by heavy trade winds blowing down from the Koolau Range. Flames raced throughout the major portion of Chinatown, and entire blocks of buildings and homes were consumed in the holocaust.

After the plague and the devastating fire, Honolulu was in ruins, and Carter's talent for organization and management was vitally needed. The city fathers practically commandeered his services. All his plans to leave Oahu had to wait until the more immediate city problems would be worked out.

Not until the plague was totally arrested did Carter take final steps to assume his new responsibilities on the Big Island. This was several months after his legal appointment had been made official. Finally, Carter sailed for Hawaii.

Alfred Wellington Carter was the son of Samuel Morrill Carter, a whaler. His mother, Harriet Layman Carter, was an extraordinary and kind woman, who maintained a tastefully furnished home with an obviously often-consulted Bible con-spicuous on the parlor table. The elder Carter had become a merchant in Honolulu, where Alfred was born on April 22, 1867.

Young Alfred was a likable boy with a lopsided grin and an off-key whistle. In his youth he worked at many jobs, helping in his father's coopering business, stevedoring, and hay and grain handling. He worked for the Bishop Bank, as well as for a printer and a publisher. He served a stint aboard ships sailing to San Pedro, California, and to Puget Sound, where he worked in a lumber mill. All this time he was gathering experience, learning how to deal with men, immersing himself in the rough-and-tumble of life.

Carter's first taste of the Big Island was when, as a young man of eighteen or nineteen, he sailed to Kawaihae aboard the steamer *Likelike*. He rode to Waimea on an unbroken mule and was invited to Mana by Mrs. Samuel Parker, Panana. He became enraptured with the place, enamored of the hospitality, and captivated by the idea of someday living there. The lush land in itself took hold of him from the very beginning. He wasn't to know that many years would elapse before he would actually someday be making his home there.

In the meantime he held many jobs and positions in Honolulu some in private business, some in government. As a young man he was offered a position in the government as secretary of the Board of Immigration and the Land Office. He accepted, worked at it, and became convinced that he wanted to practice law. The Supreme Court judges thought so well of him that they gave him a deputy clerkship. He served in that capacity for some time, then went to the mainland and attended Yale Law School. He finished the course one year sooner than the prescribed course and graduated cum laude in 1893, rated second in his class scholastically.

When he returned to Honolulu, he went into partnership with his cousin, Charles Carter, an older brother of George R. Carter, who was later to become governor of the Islands. Subsequently, Alfred formed a partnership with Lorrin Thurston and Will Kinney, two of the most prominent lawyers in Hawaii. For a while he even served as deputy attorney general, acquitting himself remarkably well in that capacity. After resigning as deputy, he was offered the position of first circuit judge. He accepted, on condition that he would not be expected to remain on the bench longer than two years.

So now in 1900, Alfred Carter arrived in Waimea as manager and controller of the Parker Ranch. He gave the ranch a thorough inspection and found it to be frightfully run-down.

His arrival had been preceded by a month of high winds; and there were troubles on the spread. Things were going badly and boded for the worst.

Little or no effort had been made to introduce new, good blood into the herds. There was little fencing, too few paddocks —next to nothing in the way of segregation. The watering conditions were abominable. The only real effort at distributing good water to the cattle was a small pipeline running down from the Kohala Mountains. Parched animals had to walk almost thirty miles to get from grazing land to water and back again. Carter was later to say, "Upon my first look at the state of the ranch, my shirt went clammy against my shoulder blades." But he was not one to cry havoc and vowed to do something about the situation.

Carter hadn't reckoned with another thing, either, Sam Parker's interest in running the ranch had waned markedly since he had lost his devoted wife, Panana, in 1894. He had become a widower at the age of forty-two, and close attention to the intricacies of running a ranch was beyond him. At least it was fortunate that the manager, Paul Jarrett, had been seeing to most of the cattle details, and trying to operate with the ranch's diminishing funds. But it would be a hard effort, to set things right again, defeat nipped at the heels all the way.

Also, to Carter's consternation he found upon close inspection that much of the land was unproductive. Land neglect had been lethal. Disintegration of the ranch's wealth and worth was evident everywhere. With the exception of Tootsie Parker, interest had waned on everyone's part. A deadly lassitude permeated the atmosphere of the whole ranch.

But Carter set to work, and in later years, he was quoted as saying, "It was the greatest challenge of my life." The condition of the cattle, the grass, the means of watering the animals, and the general facilities for ranch operation were such that Carter omnivorously read brochures, correspondence—everything that would fill him in on animal and land husbandry. Thorough to a fault, he wanted all the facts he could digest on running a cattle ranch properly and profitably.

After having carefully assessed the true condition of the ranch, and prescribed what should be done, Carter found that both Sam Parker and Tootsie Parker agreed with him. They gave him carte blanche to operate as he saw best. The employees, too, seemed to have implicit confidence in him.

Not counting the wild cattle deep in the forests, the ranch still had approximately 5,000 in the herd; and they were the result of inbred, lanky, uncared-for beasts. Carter had noticed that the steers of five years' growth would hardly average 500 pounds in dressed weight—and, commercially, that was not enough. He was also quick to note that little or no effort had been made to bring in more new blood to the animals. Observing some of the more scrawny steers, he remarked sourly, "Those wouldn't even make good glue!"

So Carter outlined a plan for fencing whereby separation and segregation could be instituted. He stipulated what he wanted in the way of blooded cattle and horses. He looked over the water situation and came up with valid suggestions on that, too.

Tirelessly, he sought sources of information on agriculture, pest control, and forestry. He had an all-consuming desire to learn. Everyone gave him complete and unreserved cooperation, and he became one of the ranch "family." Gradually things began to pick up.

There was one major hitch, however, which began to develop, and Carter found it disconcerting to his plans. Improvements on the ranch meant more expenditures, and the cash outlay naturally involved many financial corners that would have to be cut. Tootsie Parker was in complete agreement. Sam Parker, who had always been a free-wheeling spender, was told that he would have to economize. He took it in stride at first, but gradually, as time went by, and more huge outlays of cash were made for improvements, he protested.

And so it went; a syndrome of studying the problems, meeting them through repairs, rebuilding, making additions, altering, improving stock and grasses—all the things which make for a better, bigger, more efficient ranch business.

Distribution of water was one of the major problems to be worked out first. The situation was acute and promised to become more acute as the size of the herds increased. Carter could see the necessity of acquiring additional lands in order to get the needed water rights. He could also see the need of somehow getting the water across the plain to the Waikii area where the cattle were compelled to walk so many miles into Waimea to obtain water at the stream adjacent to Puuopelu.

Sam Parker concurred that it would someday have to be done, but he refused to expend any monies at that time. To back his arguments, he cited the opinion of some local surveyors to the effect that the plan was a physical hydraulic impossibility because friction in the proposed pipes would not allow water to travel all the way to Waikii. The contention was that not a drop of water could possibly drip from the pipes.

Carter was momentarily stymied, but he sent for books on hydraulics, studied them meticulously, and came up with the reassurance that his plan would actually work. He went back to Sam with his book-proven facts and insisted, "It'll work. And the improvement will pay for its cost in two or three years."

Sam Parker remained adamant.

That was the end of it until a short time afterward, when Sam came into Carter's office with a request. "I've got to have five thousand dollars," he said. "I'm going to Washington."

"You've received your share of the ranch income," said the soft-spoken manager. "Anyhow, there's no profit on hand."

When Sam mentioned simply borrowing the money, Carter changed his approach. "Tell you what, Sam," he said. "I'll go out and borrow the money myself and loan it to you if you'll consent to my putting in the pipeline."

Sam stomped around the office, glaring at Carter, and

growled, "It's a holdup proposition!" Then he barged out, grumbling about out-and-out blackmail.

But all the angry display did not stop Sam Parker from returning to Carter's office several days later and agreeing to the proposition. He was still pretty abrasive about it, harassing and haranguing, but he wanted the money.

Carter negotiated the five-thousand-dollar loan, and construction began on the pipeline. It was completed on April 14, 1902. Carter wrote later with satisfaction in his journal: "The quantity which flowed at the end of the pipe when completed was fifteen thousand, eight hundred forty gallons per twenty-four hours."

He had overridden yet one more seemingly insurmountable obstacle, and his relentless drive continued with every aspect of the ranch's administration and operation.

In 1901, under his close supervision, pure registered cattle were imported. The first importation consisted of two bulls. Carter was after aristocratic, pedigreed stock, and nothing less than that would do. As time passed, and the herds were upgraded, whole carloads of purebred, registered cattle—bulls and heifers alike—were brought in to further improve the stock. They came from the finest cattle ranches in America, and the selections were meticulously made.

From the time Carter took over, to the present day, the cattle range has been under the closest of intelligent supervision. To Carter, water and grass were synonymous. No detail was missed in the study of the cattle needs. Grasses were experimented with and cultivated according to what was best for the area, the seasons, and the movement of the herds. New findings brought on additional changes. Carter knew that, reduced to its simplest common denominator, successful beef cattle ranching amounts to growing the most grass possible—of satisfactory quality—in a given region, and turning herds into it which are adapted to the climate and which will furnish the highest efficiency in both rate of gain and quality of beef.

Despite substantial ranch gains, the relationship between Sam Parker and Alfred Carter worsened progressively. There was much conflict. Sam began seeking outside legal advice and became more and more of a thorn in Carter's side. He bucked the manager at every turn, gave him *pilikia* (trouble) in spades, just stopping short of sheer harassment.

Carter was doing an excellent job and making many concessions to Sam Parker, but the element of thanklessness persisted. One day Carter was moved to observe in frustration, "Sam, if we gave you the moon, you'd want the stars for a garnish."

An example of the situation is Carter's effort in 1903 to add to the pasturage of the ranch. He found that the Waikoloa property owned by Lucy Peabody was essential to the Parker Ranch as important grazing land—and it could be acquired. When Carter finally convinced Sam of its importance, the latter concurred and agreed to the negotiations. Carter was in the midst of working out the transaction when Sam suddenly withdrew his consent.

Carter then did the only thing that seemed feasible; he negotiated with Miss Peabody in order to get the land for his ward, Thelma. He was shortly shocked to learn that Sam was already bidding for the land in his own right and for his own purpose —excluding Thelma entirely. Carter immediately brought all his legal skills to bear on the problem and, in his astute way, soon had Sam agreeing to purchase the land for the joint interest of himself and Thelma. The purchase was made.

This was just one in a series of breaches made in the understanding which the two men seemed to have made at first. More and more, Sam resented the lessening of his personal income due to ranch expansion and improvement. He had been indulged too long. The problem developed into a running fight between him and Carter, with the latter piping in more water from the Kohalas, building paddocks and feeding pens, segregating cattle with new fencing, plus a horde of other essential improvements. The costs were heavy, but Carter hewed to the line which he had originally marked out. Finally, Sam went to his own attorneys for more advice and then to Carter with a proposition whereby he would sell his part of the ranch out-right.

Carter tried to inveigh against Sam Parker's proposal, telling him that he should retain his half of the property. Sam would have none of this argument, insisting that he was going to sell out, one way or another, to *someone.*

Carter offered six hundred thousand dollars for his share. Sam seemed to agree on the price and said he would discuss it further a little later. But it wasn't long afterward that Sam Parker made an effort to take the whole ranch over by force. By this time he was making his demands known and taking drastic steps to gain his ends. He argued that this was his right because he and his uncle, John Parker II, had been in full partnership on the holdings for a long time. Sam proceeded to take action without showing his hand.

All this aggravation was peaking in 1904, just when Carter was beginning to make real progress with the ranch. He was in Honolulu at the time of the intended takeover. Getting word of it, Carter hurried back to Hawaii via steamer and found his loyal employees still holding the fort, despite an armed posse ready to move in on them. He had a long, confidential talk with Toot-sie Parker and went into detail as to how he, Alfred Carter, intended to meet the issue. Tootsie was in total agreement with Carter on every score.

Not many hours later, a heavily armed Eben Low stalked into Carter's office and found him alone. He glared at Carter and barked, "I'm taking possession of the ranch on authorization from Sam Parker." He said he had written authority to take over as manager. Low was a relative on the Parker clan side, and it was obvious that some kind of split was coming about in Parker relationships. He stated what he and Sam intended to do.

Carter listened in his quiet way and took the risk. He refused to allow Eben to take over and intimated that he would meet force with force. "What's more," he added, "Sam's only a partner in the holdings. And I'm here to protect my ward's interest."

Low wheeled around and stormed out of the office. He hurried via horseback to where all the cowboys were camping down in the Hamakua bush. At the cattle pen he harangued the riders and told them that he would be back in the early morning to give them their orders. The *paniolos* heard him out. Then foreman Johnny Lindsey quickly sent a man back to Carter to advise him of what had happened.

There were a number of things that Carter was in no mood for right then, and revolt was at the top of the list. So, when the messenger broke the news to Carter in his office, Carter rode at once to the grouped cowboys and, despite the fact that some of them were related to Sam Parker by blood lines, he told them his story and asked them to stand up and be counted. One by one, the men began expressing their loyalty to Carter. They said they would stick by him. Carter thanked them for their show of support. These were men he felt he could count upon. The men seemed placated.

Just the same, Carter appreciated the seriousness of the situation, so he hurried to Kona for the purpose of obtaining an injunction against Sam and the other men in league with him. He arrived there and found that Sam had already instituted a suit in Honolulu on June 8, 1904, which, if unprotested, would take away his guardianship of Thelma Parker.

Other serious aggravations, too, were bombarding Carter about this time. Jack Low, Eben's brother, had filed suit against Carter to have him removed from his position as guardian and manager. An injunction was issued, a receiver was appointed to manage the ranch, and everything was effectively tied up.

A Mr. E. E. Conant was appointed receiver and held that position throughout the lawsuit. During the litigation, Carter received no salary but continued to direct the affairs of the ranch through correspondence with Mr. Conant. The legal snarl ran for the next two and a half years, finally winding up in the U.S.

Supreme Court. During the trial, Eben Low was the primary witness. When all testimony was finally concluded, the Court dismissed the case.

With all this strife and loss of time and profits through litigation, there still remained the deadlock between Sam Parker and Carter's ward. If Sam Parker, with his enormous arrogance, could have his way, Thelma Parker would inherit nothing.

But, after more court proceedings with their charges and countercharges, Sam wearied of the legal travail. He simply wanted out of the whole partnership. He finally brought his attorney, Breckons, the U.S. district attorney, to Carter's house in Honolulu to seek a settlement out of court. He again confronted Carter with the plan of selling his share of the ranch.

Sam dickered for a price, but Carter stuck to his original offer of six hundred thousand dollars, despite the demand for much more.

Sam Parker accepted the offer. The *pilikia* of litigation had come to an end, and both men breathed more easily.

The deal was consummated and a decree obtained through the Third Circuit Court. Carter hurried to Waimea to take formal possession of the ranch for his ward. No interisland passenger boat was currently scheduled for Kailua on the Big Island, but he prevailed upon the steamship line's president to let him charter the sugar-carrying freighter, *Helene,* for the trip. Carter had the ship stop at Kawaihae, mounted a horse, and rode to the ranch, taking formal possession. He then rode back to Kawaihae, boarded the steamer again, and returned to Honolulu.

Of course Thelma Parker's half of the ranch was in no position to come up with any large cash sum. The financial status of the ranch was still shaky and precarious. It fell to Carter's lot to somehow arrange a bank loan for the amount. His good and long-time friend, Mr. Sam Damon, owner of Bishop and Company, had once told him that his company would back him if he were ever in need. Carter remembered this and approached the banker for the required cash.

The story goes that Mr. Damon quickly agreed that he would

keep his word, but when Carter said, "I must have it today," Damon was appalled at the urgency of the request. Then, recalling Carter's integrity and great sense of responsibility, he said, "Alfred, you shall have it today." The loan was made at once.

So Alfred Wellington Carter was now again back in the cattle business, eager to go ahead and do what he could with this huge now singly owned parcel of land and all its herds. To the men on the ranch, Carter was authority incarnate, so they fell in line, and personality clashes were minimal. Still, the problems reared huge, and some seemed insurmountable.

By the time Carter did again take up permanent residence on the ranch and had taken over full active management, the strife of litigation over the property was at an end for the time being. But it wasn't until September 20, 1906, that the legal conflict was finally brought to a conclusion, and the ranch had become the sole property of Thelma Parker, who was twelve years old by this time.

It was full time on the ranch for Carter now, and the place, run-down again though it was, posed a glittering challenge for him. He had been patient through all the litigation, but now he knew there was work to do.

He became part of the ranch's everyday activities. It was common for him to be in the saddle before daylight, riding with the *paniolos* over rough terrain, working through brush and scrubs of *panini* cactus on the foothills of Mauna Kea, pushing through heavily forested areas, helping with the roundups, the brandings. He was up against towering odds, and progress was glacially slow at first.

He wrote later: "In the early days of my being on the ranch, we would start out at three o'clock in the morning and do nothing for sometimes a whole week but rope wild cattle in rough country. Tens of thousands were roped, and it made experts of those Hawaiians. A wild bull or cow will run away if it only smells a man. However, once they turn back, nothing will stop them from charging. I have seen them lift a horse and rider on their horns." But the intrepid Carter continued taking the hazardous chances, often saying, "I'd rather be a dead lion than a live mouse."

He turned back to increased study of ranching in all its aspects. Studious, analytical, and with a bear-trap memory, he retained facts. His hunger for information stood him in good stead in ranching just as it had in law—and now his knowledge of law was a tremendous asset. While accompanying the cowboys onto the range during the roping, cutting out cattle, and general herding, he studied the vast acreage to determine where new or more fencing was essential, where more and better grasses might be grown, and where the water situation could be bettered.

Carter's enthusiasm was unbounded. It was his dominant force, and it was contagious. His credo had always been that kindness resembles God the closest and disarms man the quickest. He had a habit of charming the obtuse and disarming the wary. Although he was a quiet man, his exuberance never left him. Oddly, Carter possessed a sort of counterfeit nimbleness. He looked as though he were hurrying, but he didn't really go fast. He was always carefully thinking, planning.

Among others, two outstanding *paniolos*, Palaika and Johnny Lindsey, would have given their lives for him. The first one, big Palaika, was working a rough region one day with Carter when they found a belligerent scrub bull that belonged to an adjacent ranch. Preparatory to having it removed, Palaika threw his lasso over its head, only to have the animal start charging. It prompted Carter, too, to lasso the beast to stay its wild rush. Unfortunately, Carter's mount took fright and threw him into a rocky gulch. Carter lay there, unconscious. Palaika started attending Carter, who regained consciousness and looked up, not crying out, not flinching. But every time he breathed, he made a gasping sound.

Carter was afterward to say, "When I came to I was lying on the ground. Palaika was straddling my body, giving me *lomilomi* [massage] around the heart, and the tears were streaming down his cheeks. He thought I was dying."

Carter's leg was badly broken, and he was hurt internally. To get up and walk was out of the question, so Palaika, not a huge man, put Carter across his back and carried him five miles through the rugged country to a wagon road where he put him down and went on for help.

The other top hand, Johnny Lindsey, who had developed a deep affection for the ranch manager, had been made head *luna* in 1903. He was a cheerful and uncomplicated man, buffalo-strong. He had succeeded his uncle, "Old Tom" Lindsey, who had retired due to bad health. Carter's fealty and allegiance to his employees had a habit of bringing out deep loyalty from them. He gave his men credit for intelligence. Their willingness to perform for him beyond the call of duty was proved time after time. Johnny Lindsey was a prime example, and Carter always spoke of Lindsey with deep affection.

Carter liked to talk of the time he imported the fabulous Hereford bull, Odd Fellow, to strengthen and blood up the stock. The animal was brought ashore from a ship at Hilo on the eastern side of Hawaii. The trusted Johnny Lindsey was sent to bring the bull safely to the ranch, a distance of well over fifty miles through harsh, lava-strewn country.

The trek proved almost impossible, for the massive hooves of Odd Fellow took a cruel beating, became bloody with gashes and splits. Its legs carried the beast slowly, painfully over the hard terrain. The situation got so bad that Johnny dismounted and laboriously cut up chunks of his saddle into protective shoes for the now lame bull. Thus the animal was finally brought in in fairly good shape.

Carter's largesse with the "family" members of the ranch was always generous. Fortunately, he and Tootsie Parker always saw eye-to-eye when the good of the ranch was concerned. They were a team, and their charities toward those who made up the ranch—relatives and employees alike—were substantial.

Baskets of food, plus money, were their common donations to needy families, more often than they would admit.

Carter rendered regular reports to Tootsie, giving her an accounting of his every important move, and she reciprocated. She made no objection to the limits he set for her expenditures, although she was in a position of influence, the purse strings at her fingertips. She strove to curb all unnecessary spending, totally the reverse of Samuel Parker in this regard, and her attitude was a tremendous boon to Carter and his plans. Later, when the ranch was again beginning to prosper, Carter substantially raised her spending limits.

Before a year had passed after Carter took over the ranch in 1899, he sent one of his expert stockmen to the mainland to pick out some new blood for the ranch—cattle, horses, hogs, and a few chickens. He made stipulations that, for the cattle, he wanted Holsteins, Herefords, and Durhams. In his own words, he demanded of the cattle purchases: "Pure blood, good conformation, about eighteen months or two years old."

As for horses, he insisted that the stallions were to be bought only if they were full-blooded animals of good conformation. Anything other than the best would not suffice for the Parker Ranch.

His liaison man efficiently arranged for shipment of fifty-six head of cattle, one Percheron stud, one jack, six pigs, and two dozen chickens. The start of the ranch's stock upgrading was under way. Not only was undesirable stock weeded out as early and fast as possible, but new, better stock continued to be brought in. The best blood qualities were selected. New orders to distant stock markets became more and more stringent. Carter corresponded with the top, reliable stock farms and exchanged many letters in procuring the finest of stock.

The first and most outstanding bull brought in was in 1902; it was Odd Fellow, a magnificent Hereford. The results with this bull determined Carter's subsequent interest in Herefords. He registered all ranch calves and went at the breeding of fine

stock with a dedicated zeal. True, he brought in a few short-
horns and Devons, but Herefords were his infatuation. Holsteins were brought in for the dairy herd, and they, too, were
progressively upgraded through the years.

The ranch stock improved to the point where Carter made
trips to the mainland to attend livestock shows and often had
difficulty in purchasing additional stock which could compare
with what he already had. His trips there led to excellent con-
tacts with top cattlemen, and he often entertained them at Waimea. The visiting cattlemen rhapsodized about the ranch, its
stock and its management.

To protect his investments in imported blooded stock,
Carter saw to it that the animals had special attendants to accom-
pany them en route. The hunt for better purebreds went on and
on, with the quality level on the ranch going higher and higher.
It reached a point in later years when it could be said that the
Parker Ranch herd of registered Hereford cattle was perhaps
the largest and one of the highest grade in the world. In time,
Carter brought in pureblood Herefords from Independence,
Missouri, from Eminence, Kentucky, from Wisconsin, Indiana,
and elsewhere, always picking the choicest animals from the
most select herds.

Along with the development of the ranch's pureblood herds,
Carter went deeper into investigations of the production of
forage grasses and clovers from various parts of the world. This
became a continuing interest through the years, and resulted in
bringing in Rhodes grass from South Africa, Yorkshire fog from
the meadows of England, cocksfoot from the same country,
paspalum from Australia, bluegrass from Kentucky, various clovers from different areas of the world, brooms and vetches, ryes,
pigeon peas, certain grain grasses and many other varieties.

For the most part, these were carefully tried in experimental
plots before they were sown widely on the range. The conditions of moisture, elevation, wind, and heat under which each
grew best were demonstrated. Proved types were then seeded

over the range. Among the grasses selected, perennials were preferred because they could keep producing throughout the entire year. It entailed much study and much experimenting, but it was worth it. Most of the grass-producing regions of the ranch were being made into a mat of nature's palatable food for animals, and presenting ever verdant surfaces to be cropped.

Carter carefully developed the small Holstein herds for milk purposes. He devised paddocks for the development of carefully bred mules and draft horses, plus a horse herd which ran to several thousand head. The horse herd was to produce saddle animals for the *paniolos*. He saw that the cost of raising a scrub horse was comparable to raising a thoroughbred, so he applied the same degree of scientific breeding to the horse herd as he did to the Herefords.

He made incessant trips to the United States mainland to obtain the best stallions available. Fifty thousand dollars and more for a single thoroughbred suitable for the ranch was a common price. Naturally, a few purchases went sour, but Carter learned from such experiences. As he often said, "I don't look back very often. The future is what interests me, because that's where I'm headed."

Carter's policy of raising thoroughbreds on open ranges like the Parker Ranch terrain contributed tremendously to the net result in the quality of the animal. They developed into stronger, sturdier animals than the horses raised carefully on the mainland in stables and paddocks. Unstabled until it reached maturity, the range thoroughbred had to hustle and scrounge for itself in a free-roaming life on the slopes and in the valleys. With a twelve-month growing season and an ever abundant supply of food, the animals grew large and strong-boned. They developed splendid hooves and powerful legs. Their stamina was beyond description. In time the Parker Ranch was selling colts to mainland and European race stables—quadrupedal speedsters that racked up astonishing reputations on the better tracks.

The United States Cavalry and Artillery drew heavily upon the ranch for horses, and this endorsement in itself bears evidence of the high-grade animals developed there. The great stallion, Eastertide—one of the ranch's earliest importations—is still talked of in glowing, reverent terms, and he sired many an elegant colt.

Impeccably high stock standards were sought and maintained. Most of today's Parker Ranch horses have thoroughbred blood in their veins, as well as being part Palomino, Morgan, or Standard bred. These strains gave them class, strength, intelligence, and conformation. Carter took a joy in all of them. Scores of his polo ponies played in important matches throughout the world; their speed, stamina, and intelligence were outstandiung, and Parker Ranch polo ponies brought the estate much repute and considerable money.

As for the ranch's personnel, Carter kept it basically a Hawaiian operation. Practically all his *paniolos* and other workers were Hawaiian or part Hawaiian. For the most part his workers were descendants of the people who had originally labored for the first John Palmer Parker. In a sense they were like the retainers on feudal estates of medieval times. Sons were inheriting the work of their fathers, growing into it, then in turn rearing sons to do the same thing. It made for a very special kind of ranch, unmatched elsewhere.

But with the ranch in its wholly roughshod, raw state, there was much work to be done to put the holdings on a substantially prosperous basis. There ensued years of backbreaking effort to bring this about. To begin with, Carter had to occupy himself with a boundary situation and endless fencing. Surveyors were brought in to ascertain and mark the true lines of the ranch. Cattle had roamed unrestrictedly in open, wild country in the past, and the mixing of the herds had developed an inferior mass of animals. The prime need was that of fencing, and much of it involved working through the roughest, most snarled sections of the ranchland.

As the grazing and pasture lands were laid out, posts were cut in the nearby forests of mamane trees and hauled directly to where the postholes were dug. Countless loads of posts were wagoned in, but where the terrain was too difficult, they were dragged by mounted *paniolos*. When the topography was too steep, strong Japanese ranch hands carried the posts on their backs. In this manner, miles of fences were constructed across, up, and down the slopes of Mauna Kea.

By February 1908, all the mountain fencing needed at the time was completed. Also, additional badly needed pipelines were installed. The ranch had been divided into three sections and additional paddocks had been erected. Then attention turned to fencing the sheep range.

All this required literally miles of wire and untold cords of posts. The precipitous canyons and steep gulches made the fencing a major problem. To compound the troubles, fencing was constantly being washed out by storm waters rushing down ravines, gullies, and gorges. Too often trespassers and interlopers deliberately cut the wire fences and broke down gates to let in their own cattle for better grazing. There was much reforestation, and it was mandatory to erect additional fences to shut off the herds from new tree growths. The prodigious fencing problems of the Parker Ranch over the years is a saga in itself. A mere glance at the map of this vast range which had to be fenced in is enough to convince any reader.

Alfred Wellington Carter was now operating a taut ranch. He expanded it, made innovations, built up good will within and without the ranch, sparked the whole machine, made it go —and kept it going. Most important of all, he remained faithful to a trust. He hewed to the policy of picking up additional important lands in fee simple. To him it made obvious good sense. Leases and rentals, he felt, were of too temporary a nature for the dynasty he wanted to keep on building and developing. There was always the danger that an expiring lease might not be renewable; higher bidders could cut you out; reluctant owners might want to take over the land themselves. Either of these happenings could leave thousands of cattle without adequate grazing pastures or water sources. Too, one could erect more permanent structures on ground which was owned, not leased. When Carter put down roots, he put them down to stay.

Some of the leases on government lands were already expiring, a worry to Carter. In instances where he was compelled to lease rather than purchase, he treated the acreage as if the Parker Ranch had full title of ownership to it. The fencing, watering, seeding, and resting were as carefully and faithfully administered as though the land belonged to the ranch.

Carter's study and usage of land on Hawaii encountered more complexities and problems than one would suspect. Much of the Big Island had been turned into a vast wasteland by molten lava, which permits little or no growing things. The Tax Office has recorded certain areas of land so barren that the rate of grazing value is twenty-five acres to one head of cattle. One head to fifty acres actually applies in certain barren regions. It happens that three acres of good pasture land per year to one head of cattle is the recognized need, and Carter had to keep this in mind in a land so laid waste by volcanic ash and lava. With increasing herds, he naturally had to increase his pasturage. The days of letting wild cattle roam at will were past in a day when a well-fed marketable steer necessarily had to furnish 600 to 650 pounds of beef.

By the time Carter was well into the problems of Parker Ranch at the turn of the century, he decided to make sheep raising an important facet of the whole ranch project. In 1904 he arranged for the purchase of the Puuloa Sheep Ranch (known today as the Keeaumoku area of Parker Ranch) from the Macfarlane estate, which included approximately 6,000 sheep and 175 head of cattle grazing at the time. He paid $20,000 for the estate, and that very year shipped 10,000 pounds of wool to Boston. In 1908 he shipped 30,000 pounds. It was a growing and salubrious deal for the ranch, and by 1912 he was compelled to order a wool press from Sydney, Australia.

From time to time he also continued to add select rams for breeding. Because of embargoes, some rather odd shipping routes had to be taken in order to import some of the animals. In one instance a select ram was shipped from Australia to Hawaii, but it had to first make a stop at New Zealand. A shipment of sheep from Australia, consigned to Hawaii, had to first go to San Francisco, and then be reshipped to Hawaii. These were just some of the minor problems with which Carter had to contend in the sheep business, but he met them all head-on just so long as it was to the Parker Ranch gain.

By astute purchasing of better sheep stock, plus improved ranch operation, the amount of wool clip per animal was vastly stepped up. The quality of the wool, too, was bettered as time went by, and it was not long before substantial amounts of top-grade wool were being shipped to the mainland's East Coast.

There seemed to be no end to Carter's proclivity for experimenting. Shortly after the turn of the century he turned his attention to the limited dairy project he had set up at Pali-okapapa, a few miles from Mana. The approximately 150 cows making up the dairy herd in 1903 were sufficient to furnish Hilo and some surrounding areas with butter. Too, his hogs waxed fat on the skimmed milk. However, in the overall ranch picture the dairying had been a minor part. But now he saw fit to increase the size of his dairy herd and step up the whole milk operation. He studied silo catalogues, subscribed to dairying publications—governmental and privately printed—and came up with tangible plans to enlarge his own dairy activities.

By 1911 he had over a hundred acres at Waimea planted to feed for his dairy herd. At Waikii he had 1,500 acres planted to corn, in addition to a large area in wheat and alfalfa. At Makaha-lau he had more corn put in and had increased the space at the dairy itself. Although silos had been constructed and used on the ranch, they proved unsatisfactory and were discontinued. Butter continued to be made, but the lack of satisfactory transportation facilities made the marketing of it very difficult and costly.

However, the dairying continued despite many handicaps, and the whole project proved feasible. The making of cheese was experimented with, and this, too, was added to the ranch's operations. It developed into a lucrative item and became a regular export to Honolulu. Although the original dairy was at Paliokapapa, it was later set up at Puukikoni, which was more adjacent and convenient to ranch headquarters.

Along with the dairying, several other ranch ventures were entered into on an ever increasing scale. They included the raising of hogs, poultry—and even bee culture. All of the products, of course, were designed for local and outer Island consumption. Berkeshire were the chosen breed for the swine, purebred chickens were brought in from the mainland, and the local turkeys were bought by the local markets. As for the bee venture, much of the coastal area from Puako to Kawaihae has a great natural growth of alagaroba, made to order for bees. Carter bought into the region and in 1903 installed equipment and bees there. It was a successful move, and a high grade of marketable honey has since been produced on the ranch.

By 1912 Carter was in need of more pasture lands for his expanding cattle herds, so he bought the Kahuku land. This was property described as extending "from sea level to the slope of Mauna Loa to an altitude of thirteen thousand five hundred feet, and containing one hundred eighty-four thousand acres."

Ninety thousand dollars were paid for this land. For so sizable a parcel, this might sound like very little, but the many lava flows of years gone by had so devastated whole regions that about one hundred and forty thousand acres were considered worthless. The real value of the land lay in *kipukas*—small areas of pasture land surrounded by old and hardened lava flows. These *kipukas* furnished extremely lush pastures.

So, new land was added to the already sprawling Parker acreage. Carter discussed such major decisions as this with Thelma (now nineteen years old) and her mother. And there was no solid assurance that Carter could renew the leases on government land which presently held so much Parker cattle. But with property values climbing, he was sure he was making a good deal. The Kahuku lands were immediately fenced, planted, stocked, and water installations set up.

Another huge stretch of land was added to the Parker Ranch on March 3, 1914. This time it was the Humuula Sheep Station, leased from Sam Parker, Jr. Carter paid $111,000 for the holdings and improvements. At the same time an additional piece of land, called Waipunalei, was purchased from Sam Parker, Sr. Carter bought Waipunalei simply because he needed the precious water which was available there; or, as he worded it: "Valuable on account of the water in the gulch."

The Humuula Station land was already stocked with some 400 head of horses, 500 head of cattle, and 23,000 head of sheep. It was basically sheep country, and Carter wanted it for that purpose. Again the move was made with the wholehearted approval of both Thelma and Tootsie. Carter assured them, after close inspection, that the sheep were superior, the cattle excellent under the circumstances, and, although there were quite a few scrub horses in the lot, there were many which would be salable to the United States Army. Carter felt that it would be a mistake to let the ranch fall into the hands of other owners and was satisfied with the purchase. He did have to contend with one problem, though. Sheep scab broke out on a large scale among the animals, and he had to resort to arsenic dip to eliminate it. The cost in man-hours and market delay was huge, but the Humuula investment still proved to be a wise one. Large shipments of profitable wool were soon being sent to the mainland.

So the efficient and aggressive Carter was relentless in rebuilding and enlarging the ranch, with its already new dimensions and proportions. The job looked staggering, but the challenge was there and he didn't back off. He bought up parcel after parcel of adjacent land until the holdings aggregated some 34,000 acres, all in fee simple. But even this did not satiate the dreams and ambitions he had for the ranch. It was only a stepping-stone to the acquiring of an additional 296,000 acres. The ranch area rose to a total of 330,000 acres in fee and reached onto the high shoulders of the extinct volcano Mauna Kea. Good grazing land, plus water, had proved to be the very essence of successful cattle raising.

Carter instituted another innovation with reference to land. From the start he was a strong advocate of homesteading for Parker Ranch employees. Home ownership for all who desired it was his aim. And those who had not thought of putting their roots deep and permanently in the land were soon convinced that it was to their advantage to do so. All this, of course, again was with both Thelma's and Tootsie Parker's vigorous approval. With their support, Carter instigated and perpetuated the policy of sponsoring home ownership for every ranch employee who wanted to avail himself of the opportunity. Usually he advanced the down payment with no request for security. Interest was not charged when monies were loaned for building expenses. He simplified matters by deducting a small, easily payable amount of money from monthly salaries.

The acquiring of land was, in no sense, for the personal, private gain of a few; it was for the good of the many. Carter embroidered old John Parker's original dream by making the ranch larger, exotic, totally engrossing, profitable—and peopled with the families that worked it.

Water distribution was certainly one of the major problems which faced Carter on the range. And the dilemma of furnishing the cattle satisfactory pasturage loomed large. The improvement of the grade of steer was essential, to say nothing of multiplying the herds, and it all depended heavily upon good and sufficient pasturage. Much of the natural grasses were trampled out by the cattle, and vast areas were quite depleted, some of the drier regions already barren of grass. For these regions Carter imported Australian grass seeds and started his experimenting. Initially, Rhodes grass took hold well. He continued an in-depth study of all the grass literature available. Bulletins of the U.S. Department of Agriculture were sent for, and pamphlets from many other sources were solicited and carefully studied. All this led to countless samplings and a multitude of trial plantings. Carter checked them for nutritional value, for hardiness, for rapidity of growth—for every essential which would contribute to the development of fine, healthy cattle. He brought in rye, orchard grass, brome, blue grass, and several types of clover. And he was not reluctant to share his findings. When he found grasses that did well on the Parker Ranch acreage, he unstintingly sent seeds to other competitive ranches so that they might reap some of the gains.

Carter farmed the ranch, feeling that it was essential that certain crops be grown for the general good of the whole enterprise. He sent soil samples to the Department of Agriculture for analysis. Records show that oats and wheat were sown, basically for their hay content. Ekoa, which is indigenous to Hawaii, was planted extensively for cattle fodder. Alfalfa, too, was grown for the same purpose.

We know that corn became a major crop, for Carter reported in his journal that "By 1906 the corn crop exceeded every estimate." Ranch records show that in a few short years corn was freighted on a large scale to both Hilo and Honolulu. Thoroughness was Carter's forte; an example of his careful analysis of ranch results is that in 1912 he had his foreman, Vredenburg at Waikii, hold to one side an acre each of oats, barley, and wheat in order to check their respective seed yields. Not content with stopping at these crops, Carter experimented with soybeans, pigeon peas, and even such fruit trees as apple, citrus, and plum.

With all the planting of grasses, plus the entry into agriculture, plant pests would have to be combated. German ivy, a pestiferous killer of grass and trees, ravaged wide areas and caused vast damage. Scores of ranch hands were employed over the years just to hold the ivy in check. There were other plant villains that had to be constantly fought; thistles, burrs, o-i, and air plants caused much harm until brought under control. Cactus was a scourge, as were the lantana and guava growths which had to be hacked out with mattocks. Thimbleberry (*akala*) spread with a rapacity that took much mattock work to keep in line. By 1912 Carter was spending as much as two thousand dollars a month to fight it. He finally won out.

Then there were various insect pests with which the ranch had to contend. Particularly the cutworms (*poko*) developed into a foe of agriculture. Carter resorted to poison spray in great quantities to combat the pest. Records of 1912 also point out that the fruit fly was taking a heavy toll of crops. Again it took poison sprays to combat the problem.

From the start, Carter looked into the possibilities and feasibilities of importing parasites to destroy plant pests, but he faced hard and fast rules from the Department of Agriculture. The Department was strongly opposed to the importation of parasites, an opposition predicated on the possibility that the parasites themselves might become a hazard in their own right. The restrictions of the Department of Agriculture made it particularly difficult for Carter and his hands to get rid of cactus.

At first the corn planting was a disaster, due to the heavy flocks of pheasants which ranged the fields. But Carter opened up the area to hunters, who materially cut down the pheasant population. However, this method of protection had to be carried out with particular care, for the noise of firearms alarmed the cattle, and their hides were occasionally peppered with shot. Hunters also increased the fire hazard, and the pheasant-shooting parties had to be closely checked and supervised.

As for forestry on the Parker Ranch—in fact on all of the Island—Carter made every effort to cooperate with the American Forestry Association. He became a member of the Association in 1902 and was later appointed to the Board of Commissioners. When the Bureau of Agriculture and Forestry was set up in the Territory of Hawaii, the Big Isle received very special attention, and Carter worked hand in glove with the Bureau. He recommended Upper Kawaihae and Puukapu as reserves and made tours of the Island with men of the Bureau so that additional reserves could be set up and protected. In the interim, he brought in tree seeds of several kinds to plant where they would do the most good. These were mostly eucalyptus, Monterey cypress, and Japan cedar. Thousands of seedlings were given gratis to other landowners. In fact, at one point the ranch was setting out seedling trees at the rate of 10,000 a week. They set a goal of 200,000—and accomplished it.

This kind of ranch and governmental cooperation became a regular thing throughout the years, and the combined effort led to the reforestation of the Kohala Mountains, thus tremendously improving the watershed there.

In 1909 Alfred Carter saw fit to establish the Hawaii Meat Company, a cattlemen's cooperative, in the interest of Hawaii cattle ranchers who were sorely beset by the Inter-Island Steamship Company's lack of cooperation on shipping stock. The carrier's steamers often neglected to pick up cattle ready for delivery at port. There were additional problems involving the carrier's bad handling of stock. The current monopoly, the Metropolitan Meat Company, was uncooperative despite taking hefty profits and declined to take deserving cattlemen into partnership.

In Carter's own words, "My idea was this; that seven of us, including the Parker Ranch, Greenwells, Maguires, Hinds, Horner, Puakea and Shipman, should buy out the property of the Metropolitan Meat Company and conduct the business as a wholesale one, leasing the present retail shops to butchers and supplying them with beef."

Carter took a steamer to Kauai, where he negotiated with George Wilcox for suitable land outside Honolulu. His plan was to do his own slaughtering and compete with Metropolitan. The property he hoped to acquire would accommodate feeding pens and a slaughterhouse. Fearing competition, Metropolitan offered to sell out to Carter's combine. The deal was concluded, and the Hawaii Meat Company was formed, with Carter in the executive capacity of president. Years later, in 1937, the company was accepted as a member of the American National Livestock Association. Except for a one-year interim in 1917, Carter held the presidency until his death. He never received any remuneration for his manifold duties with that company.

Henceforth the Hawaii cattlemen worked together in harmony. Their shipments of beef were made with few or no hitches, with Parker Ranch invariably giving way to other ranches when there was a shortage of shipping room.

But the Inter-Island Steamship Company didn't cease its uncooperative and unobliging policy. It continued to aggravate the ranchers' problems. Carter took the alternative of negotiating with a firm in San Francisco and purchased a freighter, the *Bee*. When it went into service between Hawaii and Honolulu, it immediately developed into a busy and lucrative venture. The vessel was appropriately named, and was such a prosperous investment that Carter arranged for the building of a steel freighter, the *Hawaii*. This, too, was successfully indoctrinated into the cattle hauling business. The ship, was ultimately sold to Inter-Island, but with the proviso that it would be operated wholly under Carter's control—an arrangement which was adhered to for many years.

The *Bee* was shipwrecked and abandoned on a reef off the coast of Maui in April, 1924. Carter immediately ordered another steamer from San Francisco. This vessel, the *Hornet*, stayed in operation until July 1925, when she was taken out of service. Others resumed the shuttling from island to island. The freighter problem was, in a sense, a peripheral duty for Carter, but he handled it with his usual aplomb and efficiency.

Supervising the transportation phase of ranch management involved problems arising from accidents to cattle and personnel, ship groundings, collisions, and a host of other unforeseen, unpredictable events. Carter watched the company ships with an alert, efficient eye, for he was, by family line, a man of the sea himself. His relationship with the various vessels' officers and crews was always friendly and fair. He had a particular fondness for the men who manned the steamer, *Humuula*—a ship owned and operated not by the Hawaii Meat Company but by the Inter-Island people. The *Humuula* was a vessel put in service in 1929 and constructed specifically for the shipping of cattle. The builders had taken Carter's advice as to the vessel's design and had everything constructed to order. The *Humuula* had given excellent service, and a fine friendship had been built up over the years between her captain and Carter. Captain Punahoa, widely known as "Captain Willie," was one of Carter's staunchest supporters.

Of course, in those early days the *paniolo* was still the backbone of the ranch's operation, and the cattle were the product. For the most part, the herds were made up of the longhorn stock from Mexico and the southwestern United States. The brandings took place at the renowned stone-walled pen called Puuhihale, outside of Waimea, always a place of noise and excitement.

People from far and near came to see the legerdemain as displayed by cowboys with their lariats and sure steeds. The audiences could expect anything. Wild steers often went berserk and gave the *paniolos* a lot more trouble than they could handle. In the melee, more than one cowpuncher with flower-bedecked hat would be unhorsed and have to run for the cover of the stone wall. Often a brother *paniolo* would be his rescuer, quickly picking up the downed horseman and riding him to safety. Those beasts were a far shout from the advent of the peaceful Hereford stock later introduced in a large way.

Getting the cattle to the port at Kawaihae was a project in itself. On shipping days the *paniolos* would arise about midnight, have their coffee at the ranch, then ride three miles to the big pen at Puuiki, where the steers had been driven the previous day. Then, taking advantage of the cooler night air, they would drive the herd to the beach, arriving at dawn or a little after.

That was trail's end. From the shore the cattle were driven into open pens where they could be removed as needed.

All the shipping was done out of the little village of Kawaihae. It was really nothing more than a few houses, the cattle pens, a small tidal pool, a tiny post office, a courthouse, a jail, and some ramshackle pens where the old Hawaiians kept pigs. On the beach, as well as at anchor, were fishing canoes and skiffs, while fringing the shore were stubby *kiawe* growths laden with nets drying in the sea breezes.

Small steamers plied between the Islands, and their decks carried thousands of Parker Ranch cattle. The primitive method of getting the animals aboard ship still prevailed, and top *paniolos* had to be combination cowmen and seamen.

But the hard work of wrestling cattle into the surf, tying their heads to the sides of longboats, then floating them to a ship's boom where they were lifted aboard had ended a long time ago. Parker Ranch *paniolos* today find it a lot easier and safer. The animals are now trucked to the pier, then chuted aboard barges the way they are chuted into a paddock.

The end of the old era came suddenly. On April 25, 1952, word was flashed to shore that the big steamer *Humuula* was in distress off the nearby island of Kahoolawe. The vessel was taken in tow and hauled to Honolulu. The crippled ship never resumed cattle transporting, and after a particularly disaster-fraught voyage to Florida, the *Humuula* wound up as something of a ghost ship in Floridian waters.

This, coupled with excellent interisland air travel the year round, practically marked the end of an era for passenger ship accommodations. Interisland freight ships were practically relegated to disuse because the bigger mainland freighters began delivering cargoes directly to outer Island ports, and the need for interisland freight carriers just about vanished. In their place came the many seagoing tugs with their cargo-laden barges.

The remembered S.S. *Humuula* days are talked about a lot

today by old-time *paniolos*. The combined cattle, freight, and passenger vessel was the busiest of all territorial carriers. She lugged imports and exports of manifold kinds: fruits, vegetables, fabricated materials, bricks, tile, and lumber. Automobiles also became one of her important cargoes. There were other freighters, like the S.S.*Hawaii* and the *Bee*, but the *Humuula* became the workhorse of the group.

The early Kawaihae port activities are of the most interest when reminiscing today. The husky *Humuula* was constructed basically for the shipping of cattle from the outer Islands to Oahu, and she carried the lion's share of Parker Ranch cattle. Named after the Parker Ranch Humuula Sheep Station, she was a seaworthy ship of 961 tons, 210 feet in length, and with a 38-foot beam. She had 2,000-H.P. geared turbine engines, which could thrust her along at thirteen to fourteen knots an hour.

Prior to 1937 there was no wharf at Kawaihae, and the *Humuula* had to drop anchor offshore and wait to be serviced by the *paniolos* from the beach. Powerful workhorses of Percheron extraction were utilized for herding the cattle into the surf and getting them lashed to the whaleboats in deeper water. A mounted *paniolo* found it could be quite a chore to swim a cantankerous steer or cow through the surf to the waiting whaleboat.

At that point the seagoing *paniolo* would toss a loop over the animal's snout, bring the rope up the cheek, and make another loop around the head. In this way the animal's head was well out of the water, it could breathe freely, and the buoyancy of its body kept it afloat. Back and forth, the horse and rider would shuttle, bringing a steer each time to the whaleboat. When the sea was kicking up, it became a hard-swimming fight.

Once the animals were head-tied, six on each side of the whaleboat, a motorboat towed the whole increment seaward to the mother ship. There, the cattle were lifted by a belly sling into the air by the steamer's hoist, then deposited on deck for further transportation.

In earlier years before cattle were dehorned, and antedating the introduction of hornless or poled cattle, the animals were lashed by their horns to the railings set up on the cattle deck to avoid the danger of injury or bruising. However, in later years most of the cattle were hornless and left free but tightly packed in bulkheads that amounted to small, individual paddocks. Additional care was given the animals during the loading by constantly spraying them with cooling water. Their exposure to the sun at sea level was a far cry from their habit of grazing on the high, crisp slopes of Mauna Kea. In short, the seagoing cowboys aboard ship had all the knowhow of the *paniolos* who plied their trade ashore, and they knew how to deliver the animals in prime shape at Honolulu. Their whooping and shouting and handling of cattle at sea differed little from that of their counterparts on land.

10

A Time of Prosperity

and Death

THELMA had been raised by Tootsie Parker as if she were not an heiress at all. Her tastes were simple, her interests catholic, and she had become an omnivorous reader. Many common household duties were given her, and she was rapidly developing into a young woman with all the graces of a person of her thoroughbred background.

The relationship between Samuel Parker and Carter had improved. The two men were far apart in their thinking, but somehow a kind of truce was being maintained. In 1904 Colonel Sam Parker (the colonelcy had been conferred upon him by King Kalakaua) married the wealthy widow of James Campbell —Mrs. Abigail Campbell. His own wealth didn't compare with that of his new bride, but he did have all the social graces and an entree into the best social circles. After the wedding reception in Honolulu, the city's leading newspaper reported that the affair was "The most brilliant social event in Honolulu history to date."

The year 1906 saw the end of the long and bitter conflict over Thelma's ownership of half the Parker Ranch. The sale of Sam Parker's half to her had given her full reign over the ranch. Both her mother, Tootsie and Alfred Carter were delighted that all the trying litigation was well behind them.

The ranch now became Carter's very life. When Tootsie and Thelma were at Puuopelu and not in San Francisco, Carter watched out for their interests, protecting them, and remaining ever alert to their comforts and pleasures. It was a time of increasing prosperity for the ranch. Carter was able to look out over the ranch's expanse and say, "Out of the mud blooms a rose!" Still, Carter had to continue fighting with the ranch's cattle problems, water problems, grass problems, and all the other difficulties which beset so huge an undertaking. But under his excellent guidance, the barometer of success continued upward. He was now riding the crest of a huge ocean wave of prosperity.

In 1911 Tootsie decided to take Thelma, now seventeen, to Europe. The two of them had been invited to the coronation of King George V in late June 1911. Thelma was enthralled with the idea, and, best of all, the ranch's prosperity could well absorb the expense of the trip. They sailed, saw a king crowned, and had the rare pleasure of meeting royalty from all over the world.

By 1912, when Thelma had come of age, even greater prosperity was upon the Parker Ranch—still thanks to the vision, talent, and resourcefulness of Alfred Carter. He had welded a strong, loyal group of people around him, and the results were gratifying in every direction. But there was one facet of the picture with which he as not satisfied, and that was the education of the young people. Before the ranch could afford it, Carter had often dug down into his own pockets and paid the school tuition for young persons whom he thought deserving. As Thelma's trustee, he now took advantage of the ranch's new prosperity and set up a policy whereby a certain percentage of the ranch profits would go for benevolent and educational purposes. He felt that the tiny school at Waimea was inadequate for the outstanding and more promising children in the area. So, Carter arranged to send many of the more promising children to the

Kohala Seminary, to the Hilo Boarding School, and to Kamehameha at Honolulu.

Carter saw, too, that the Parker Ranch benefited church work in Waimea. With Thelma's and Tootsie's full approval and help, he arranged for aid to the Catholic, Mormon, Congregational, and Episcopal churches. As for their many benefit *luaus* (feasts), the ranch supplied great quantities of beef and pig. Nor did the Parker Ranch benevolence stop at this. Liberal donations and encouragement were given freely to Scout, YMCA, YWCA, school groups—any and all youth factions which came within the orbit of Waimea. It goes without saying that the elders, too, were taken care of whenever there was need. Even when hospitalizations were essential in Honolulu, the needy were not denied. When "ranch family" needed attention or help, it received it immediately. Alfred Carter, Tootsie, and Thelma were truly an oasis of help, good sense, and humility to those in need.

Thelma had blossomed into a sensitive girl, deep-feeling like her mother. Back from Europe, Thelma rode with the *paniolos* over the range. The air was good with the hovering smell of crushed grass. She was happy. She and Tootsie occupied Puuopelu and entertained their many guests from the other Islands, as well as from the mainland. It was a scintillating social whirl. And life was good.

After a year at school, Thelma sailed with her mother for the Islands once more. During the voyage she met a handsome young Henry Gaillard Smart.

The captain intoduced Gaillard Smart as a Virginian on his way to Honolulu to take up a position with the Trent Trust Company. Smart's courteous manner with them was the thing which first caught the attention of Thelma and her mother. It developed that he was the son of Dr. Richard Davis Smart and Ella Gaillard Aiken Smart, the former an eminent theologian of the Methodist Church. This was no ordinary cruiseship romance. It was based on deep understanding and genuine mutual admiration. The voyage to the Islands opened doors to two young people who seemed wholly made for each other.

The two were married at Puuopelu on July 25, 1912. The ceremony was an exotic event with Puuopelu's big salon decked with masses of flowers and filled with well-wishers. Thelma herself was a study in rare beauty, grace and charm in a shimmering white satin wedding gown with sleeves of Brussels lace. Following the ceremony, the whole ranch reverberated with celebration over its little mistress having reached womanhood and happily married bliss.

Then an additional dimension, and reason for further celebrating, occurred on the ranch when on May 21, 1913, Richard Palmer Smart was born to the newlyweds. Tootsie Parker and Carter themselves took deep delight in the fact that a fine young male heir would someday head the ranch. There were parties and *luaus*, and it was as though a prince had been born to a queen.

Before the now toddling little Richard was a year old, Thelma and Gaillard Smart were preparing for a trip to Europe. She was particularly anxious to revisit some of her favorite haunts in Paris and share the joys of them with her husband. As for himself, Gaillard wanted to look into the feasibility of importing foreign cars and agenting them to an American clientele. Although Thelma was now pregnant again, she did not intend to let that stand in the way of their travel plans. Like her great-great-grandfather, her confidence and courage knew no bounds. In fact, she even intended to take along her firstborn, Richard, who was little more than nine months old.

So, early in 1914 the Smarts sailed for France, their hopes high. But Thelma became ill shortly after arriving in Paris. With all France threatened by invasion from without, and major countries vying for some kind of a balanced power, the Smart junket had been caught in a tense place at a taut time.

Thelma's condition worsened and she had to be hospitalized. A baby daughter, Elizabeth Ella, was born to her—and both mother and child were not doing well. The Smarts appeared to be inescapably trapped, for the European situation was worsening by the hour. Gaillard was warned by friends, but now with a seriously ill wife in the hospital and a newborn baby even more ill, quick flight from Europe was utterly impossible.

Then during those first days of August 1914, the Germans struck. A friend and member of the diplomatic corps came to Gaillard once more and stressed the imminent danger which faced the Smarts. Other friends, too, emphasized the menace of these frenzied days.

Finally, despite their desperate personal straits, the Smarts fled to Le Havre with their two children and a nurse. Within an hour before the gates of Paris were slammed shut by the war, Gaillard took his little family aboard the S.S. *Imperator* and sailed for the United States. All exodus from Paris had been halted. The escape had been a narrow one, and now there was the new risk of being on a ship when Thelma required hospitalization. By this time both the young mother and the newborn baby were in very delicate condition.

Upon arrival in the United States, the whole Smart family seemed on the verge of total collapse. The baby died in New York. Thelma was transferred to Virginia, where Gaillard's parents had a summer home, and her malady was diagnosed as tuberculosis. This was in an era when the medical profession had pitifully limited control over the ravages of the disease, and Gaillard was told privately that his wife's case was terminal, that she had but a few months to live.

Gaillard was not a well man himself at the time, and the shocking news of his wife's condition was traumatic, to say the least. Reluctantly, Smart sent word of the situation to Tootsie in California. Thelma's mother entrained at once for Virginia to join them and do what she could. Upon her arrival, it was decided that the soft, friendly clime of the Islands might be the one therapy which would save or, at least, prolong Thelma's life. Hawaii could be all things to her.

They chanced the trip. Gaillard Smart and Tootsie accompanied the ailing girl westward, but they got no farther than San Francisco befor her health got progressively worse. Thelma was never to go home alive.

Ironically, Thelma's one last taste of Hawaii had to be a vicarious one, although a generous one. A group of Hawaiian musicians was currently performing at the San Francisco Exposition of 1914, and as soon as the musicians heard of Thelma's plight, they came daily to Tootsie's home and sang beneath Thelma's window. Aching with longing, yet laced with sheer willpower, she closed her eyes and drank in the music of Polynesia. The musicians played and sang all her favorite songs of the Islands, and her final days were at least flavored with sweet, nostalgic memories. Each softly strummed ukulele brought back girlhood memories. She died in the late fall, her beloved Islands still 2,500 miles to the west.

Tootsie and Gaillard were bewildered and numb. They would never again hear the whole-throated laughter of their Thelma. They could only think back on her with grief in their hearts. Fortunately, the motherless boy, Richard, was something to cling to, part of the deceased Thelma.

Thelma's body was taken back to Hawaii and laid to rest in the family cemetery at Mana. The sorrow of the *paniolos* and other ranch hands and their families was like a specter over the ranch. No one could quite comprehend why such a fresh, gay, and loving young woman should go to so early a grave. Alfred Carter himself was inconsolable. So much of his planning, building, and sweating, it seemed, had been for the winsome, beautiful Thelma Parker Smart. But he carried on.

As for the young widowed husband, he was despondent. There was his young son, Richard, to look after—but Gaillard was already almost too sick to do that. Eleven months later, in November, 1915, Gaillard died of meningitis at the home of his parents.

The series of tragic events shook Tootsie's very soul. She was just about bereft of all things important to her; her daughter was gone, an infant granddaughter, and now her beloved son-in-law —all taken from her in the space of a year. Had Tootsie not had bottomless courage, she might easily have fallen apart herself. But the one redeeming feature of all the recent days for her was the fact that she was left with her grandson, Richard Smart, whom she adored. He became her one solid joy. She accepted him as her charge, dedicated herself to raising and training him in the same fashion as his mother would have. Richard would be a Parker, first, last, and always.

As for Carter, he went on with the ranch development; the man pushed on to make his dreams come true. Like Tootsie, he was a practical person, and he numbed his sorrow with work. There was still a dynasty to hold together, a ranch to maintain, develop, and improve. Many people were counting upon him, and he felt the responsibility.

11

Two Wars and the

Modern Age

THE YEAR 1914 was an austere experience for all of Parker Ranch. Shipping was tied up, supplies were short, manpower was down, the country's economy was awry, and Carter was compelled to make drastic changes in his mode of operation. All the enthusiasm of the past several years had proved to be unjustified euphoria.

In September the Australian government halted the exporting of all beef. The problem then of supplying local military with beef fell strictly to Hawaii's cattlemen. It also meant that selling all its beef output to the military would entail a loss of thousands of dollars per month. Beef necessarily had to be brought in from California to take up the slack. With the beef situation becoming progressively more acute, Carter had to employ even more efficient methods of ranching whereby he could raise more stock, fatten the animals faster, and get things done with more rapid dispatch.

Alfred Carter had to contend with an avalanche of directives from the government; large operations like his were to pay their taxes on or before due dates; he must furnish the Food Commission all the facts and figures on the kinds of livestock he could

Paniolos transferring cattle from beach to freighter, through the surf at Kawaihae

John Palmer Parker III

Alfred Wellington Carter

At right, Elizabeth Jane Dowsett Parker
(Aunt Tootsie)

Henry Galliard Smart, on the grounds at Puuopelu

Aunt Tootsie

Thelma Parker

Annie Thelma Parker Smart
as a bride

Thelma Parker Smart and
her son Richard

Aunt Tootsie and young Richard

Richard Palmer Smart

Snow covered Mount Mauna Kea, as seen from the Parker Ranch

Paniolos and the remnants of volcanic cones on the Ranch land.

possibly supply; there would be no slaughtering of calves, cows, or sows; rather, they should be retained for breeding. It was a hectic time, and Carter had to bring every faculty to bear on it.

Then, as if Carter and the ranch people were not already contending with enough extracurricular duties and doubled-up work, that vicious cattle disease, anthrax, hit with a vengeance. In that there had been no previous evidence of anthrax on the ranch or on any of the neighboring islands, plus the fact that it had now hit right after the beginning of the 1914 war, there was reason to believe that the enemy had planted germs in the soil. Too, cattle on Kauai had suddenly been attacked by the same disease at the same time. With the Parker Ranch being almost the sole source of beef for the local army and civilian population, the Island cattle industry was a natural and logical enemy target.

Carter tried to convince the district attorney at Honolulu to cable Washington for help. He could get no authority to take precautionary measures against outside sabotage. So Carter on his own responsibility—and with the danger of prosecution—stationed armed guards at every entrance to the ranch property. No one was allowed to enter before a thorough inspection had been made. Later, Carter admitted, "It was a high-handed action, but it worked effectively."

It took much time and great effort to control the anthrax problem and stamp it out. And it will probably never be known whether or not Carter's stopgap measures at the ranch entrances were the right answers. But direct action was his motto, and once again he resorted to the only tactics he knew.

On top of all this, Carter and other responsible people on the ranch like Tootsie promoted the sale of War Saving Stamps, made the Red Cross Drive a success in the district, and pushed Liberty Bonds. In the Red Cross efforts, the Parker Ranch attained the highest record of the whole Island. Carter's personal purchases, along with those of many Parker employees, lifted Liberty Bond sales to many thousands of needed dollars.

The ranch ably furnished the cavalry and artillery with fine, durable horses. Carter stepped up the ranch's agricultural products output to an all-time high. Two thousand acres of corn were sown in 1916. Carter doubled that figure in 1917. By 1918 the ranch began the production of cornmeal. This required the importation of special machinery, which was costly, but the results were gratifying.

Patriotism was such that a troop of ranch cowboys was formed, called the Waimea Cavalry, a crack outfit trained eagerly for combat action in the European war zone. But combat never materialized; their fine horsemanship and weaponry was to no avail, for the whole troop was ultimately transferred to the Island of Oahu in 1918 and stationed at Kawailoa for the duration.

With the capable and wise Alfred Carter as the guiding light, Parker Ranch contributed its part to the war effort. After the Armistice of 1918, a return to normalcy was instituted under his sage administration, and once more the stress was on ranch expansion, development and improvement. Within five years vast changes were wrought, for the restrictions of war were at an end. By 1923 several aspects of the ranch had changed startlingly.

The years slipped by; it was a period of acquiring even more land and more stock. One of the best investments for the Parker Ranch was Alfred Carter's purchase of the Kohala Ranch in June 1932. It was acquired from the heirs of the Woods Estate and was bought for $240,000. It contained a cattle herd of 5,476 head and was a worthwhile addition to the other Parker holdings.

Carter did as he had done in the past and quickly, efficiently brought the addition up to Parker Ranch standards. He welded it in with the balance of the acreage and thus created an even larger acreage. Among other things, he immediately had it planted with the grasses which were already doing so well on the regular Parker pastures and ranges. In short order the Kohala lands were made an integral part of the whole scheme of things.

The following year, on March 12, 1932, Carter was appointed guardian of Richard Smart and his property, succeeding the Trent Trust Company in this office. This was just one more measure of the esteem in which Tootsie continued to hold the now graying Alfred Carter. To the old gentleman this appointment was sacrosanct, and he was proud of his new responsibility. As an aside, it might be noted that in May of the next year, 1933, when Carter's ward Richard Smart became of age (twenty years old) he drew up a power of attorney, making Alfred W. Carter and his son A. Hartwell Carter attorneys-in-fact.

In 1937 A. Hartwell Carter became official manager of the ranch. He was to remain as such for twenty-three years. For a long time the father had been carefully indoctrinating the younger man, and there now developed a collaboration-type of management that would last for years on end.

These were years during which Richard Smart shuttled back and forth between Hawaii and the mainland. He wanted to be *of* the ranch in lieu of just the heir to it. His long stays on the ranch were utilized in studying the problems of the business and acquainting himself with the modern methods which Carter was continuing to install. Alfred Carter was painstaking in imparting his knowledge of ranching to the younger man, and the latter was grateful for the tutoring.

The two had much in common, and Carter was steadfast in his belief that he was dealing with an aspiring young man who had all the qualifications to make a good cattleman. Smart's love of all that made up the ranch seemed to point that way. For example, Smart thrilled at the sight of the red herds grazing on the mesas; he relished watching a straggling V-line of geese flying over, their quavering calls drifting down; he liked to be astride a fine horse at dawn and watch the new day begin; he liked the sweet pungency of the corrals and stables. Ranch work in all its aspects—whether in a fog wine-colored with sunset or under the starry Hawaiian sky—was to his liking.

But there were interim years, too, when Richard Smart persued a career as professional entertainer. Show business was also in his blood. Carter was doing so well with the ranch development that he needed no additional assistance in the management department, so Smart felt no great moral obligation to be there with the administration of things. With his theatrical background from the university, plus some theater training, he went into musical comedy and cabaret work—and with considerable success.

Another hiatus from Smart's routine came about with the advent of World War II. After enemy bombs fell on Pearl Harbor on December 7, 1941, he entered the service and became a camouflage expert in the Army Corps of Engineers. His stage and theater background now stood him in good stead, for he had something tangible and highly constructive to offer his country.

As rapidly as possible, the Islands were set up as staging areas for America's striking-back forces. The whole region was pinpointed as a logical and valuable training ground. The Carters and Richard Smart were vitally aware of the importance of the ranch's part in the war effort. A sprawling army camp was set up on the Parker Ranch in March 1942. Quonset huts and tents fringed the Parker herds, and it was a strange juxtaposition. The serene pastoral scene looked incongruous alongside the military setup.

First came the infantry, then the Marines—survivors of the bloody Tarawa battle in the South Pacific. Soon they were calling the place "Camp Tarawa." As the war progressed, more and more servicemen were brought in. The Parker Ranch military center played host to in excess of 50,000 servicemen of the United States Armed Forces.

Field maneuvers were held, and sham battles were staged. All manner of war preparations and training took place. It is ironic that much of this frenzied activity took place exactly where, centuries before, legions of Hawaiian warriors had fought and died in their own intra- and interisland conflicts. But now soldiers and Marines were playing at make-believe war that would be only too real in the months ahead. Thousands were to die later under Japanese fire on distant island beaches. Thousands would survive, and Parker Ranch lands helped contribute to their survival.

The early days preceding the Pearl Harbor attack had not left the Parker Ranch unchanged by any manner of means. In early 1940 close to two hundred of the women on the ranch were busily knitting for the Red Cross. Every possible move was being made to step up beef production to meet the gathering need for more meat. Colonel Davidson of the U.S. Army Air Corps came to Hawaii, and Alfred Carter toured with him in an effort to find suitable sites for landing fields. It was essential to have as many dispersion areas as possible.

Although the impossible lava makeup of much of the Big Isle made it an unlikely place to locate such fields, some sites were found that were adequate. They made their recommendations to Washington. Before the Pearl Harbor attack the Parker Ranch was asked by the Emergency Food Committee for Hawaii to furnish statistics on its monthly shipments of stock to Honolulu. The government certainly sensed that war could lay ahead—and the Parker Ranch would necessarily become an integral part of it.

By the time the Japanese struck at Pearl Harbor, the Islands were already deeply involved in the war effort. Defense workers and military personnel already had put a strain on Oahu with their numbers; now there were more people to be taken care of. Transportation, food, and housing were the main current needs. The interisland steamers were commandeered by the government, which vitally affected Parker Ranch and Hawaii Meat Company operations. It was difficult to find ways in which to ship beef or any agricultural products.

It took much figuring and calculating to know how to divide the ranch's production. With a mind as sensitive as a seismograph, Carter worked it out from day to day, week to week. He allotted his shipments as he saw fit, providing first for the hospitals, which he saw as top priorities. From there on, he kept his plans as elastic as possible to meet all requirements. But it meant that he had to contend with governmental red tape; military officers in many instances simply did not know or understand the problems of a ranch the size of Parker's. Their established routines often ran contrary to good cattleman sense. For example, at first they even declined to accept delivery on chilled beef in lieu of the frozen product.

The planning became time-consuming and frustrating. There was the necessity of studying, estimating, and reporting in detail all the arrangements for supplying the beef market. The ranch had to be precise in its reports and plans, for it was essential that the military know what to expect.

At the time of Pearl Harbor, Carter estimated that the cattle on Oahu could furnish the market for no more than three weeks. At the end of that period Hawaii's herds would have to be drawn upon. The inroads would be great, and the challenge would be to fulfill the demands without drawing upon the breeding stock. All this would be compounded by the fact that the steamer service was so curtailed by the military that satisfactory delivery of stock appeared impossible. It took much involved and complicated negotiating and arranging.

One of the major problems stemmed from the difficulty in finding storage facilities for frozen and chilled beef in Honolulu. This was followed by the delicate question of to whom the shipments must be ultimately distributed. There were the hospitals, the navy, the Marines, the army, the civilians, and so on.

Restrictions on gasoline, oil, and ranch supplies tied things up badly for the Parker Ranch. Again and again all important purchasing efforts were stymied or limited. The thousand-and-one wartime demands made for cumbersome going. For example, vaccination and immunization for all employees was officially ordered. Records had to be kept on all employees, and their paychecks had to indicate whether or not they had citizenship papers. The draft took many of the best ranch and slaughterhouse employees, and new hands were difficult to find due to the labor shortage.

But the troubles were not all beef troubles. There was the agricultural end of the ranch which had to meet war demands. In his zeal to increase output, Carter negotiated with officials in charge of seed distribution in Honolulu. He requested a germination test of Waikii corn and checked on other seeds, wanting the best possible results from his plantings. By 1943 over 1,700 acres of corn were planted on the Parker Ranch. And, although the war years were drought years and most crops were disappointing, the 1943 corn crop was a good one. The stalks averaged seven feet high, with two solid, excellent ears to the stalk. Despite the adverse weather conditions, Parker Ranch was coping remarkably well.

Another problem had to be faced in 1942 when an epidemic of blackleg struck the cattle. This infectious disease is usually fatal. Again there was reason to suspect that the disease might have been planted by enemy saboteurs, but there was no way of telling for certain. Carter's *paniolos* vaccinated over 4,000 calves and managed to halt the disease's further inroads.

With all this change, so, too, was life altered for Alfred Carter and Richard Smart. Smart's time was devoted to devising ways of camouflaging military installations, vehicles, weapons, and barracks. His natural creativity was put to the test and not found wanting. Carter found that managing and overseeing the ranch with all this additional complexity of military activity had become a gargantuan task, but he, too, accepted the challenge like a true Parkerite, discharging his duties with excellence. He had the extra duty, also, of entertaining, briefing, and cooperating with upper-echelon officers.

Richard Smart made an additional contribution to the war effort when he advised the Carters to give all privileges to the occupation army without cost. "Let them have it gratis," he insisted. This was done, and the War Department wound up more than a little indebted to the Parker Ranch.

But now that the war in the Pacific was at its most deadly and lethal stage, a serious complication arose for the ranch. Alfred Carter, the mainspring of the whole ranch mechanism, was going into a physical decline. In fact, in the spring of 1941 he underwent major surgery and was hospitalized for almost three months. Throughout 1942 his health continued to worsen and, with all the ranch complications, it was fortunate that Hartwell Carter was able to carry the load at this time.

In excess of 50,000 acres of the ranch were taken over by the military for war maneuvers. The area was designated as an Impact (shooting) Area, and all cattle had to be moved to safer acreage. Also, no ranch hands were allowed in the Impact Area, so new problems were created by the huge increase in cactus growth, by frequent fires, and by punctured pipelines. A heavy stand of fine trees was utterly wiped out by a single conflagration—a thing practically unheard of in previous years of ranch operation.

Oahu was a place of burgeoning shipyard activity, using up all manpower, supplies, and materiel. Consequently, the ranch was being frightfully short-changed on its own needed requirements. The Selective Service drained away the young and the strong. So there was a labor shortage, as well as materiel shortages, transportation shortages, and vehicle fuel shortages. Inter-island steamers were more heavily commandeered by the government—and the ranch was hard hit by the resultant tieup.

The beef business was definitely in turmoil, what with the government needing the meat, and the ranch's packer, Hawaii Meat Company on Oahu, being flooded with military orders. After further careful study, Carter decided to fill only 75 percent of his usual beef orders, and, of course, furnish all hospitals first.

Then began even more red tape problems with the government. Military officers who did not understand the intricacies of the beef business gave Carter unnecessary *pilikia*. And then, again compounding the problems, the slaughterhouse had to suspend operations at night on account of the blackout regulations.

But Carter's tact and strategy in all negotiations and actions kept the whole relationship with the government in working order. A 1943 letter in from the U.S. Engineers Office in Hilo read: "*Mahalo* [thanks] for the equipment that you made available for use in defense projects, Hawaii. It would have been impossible for this office to perform the many different jobs required, without the *kokua* [help] of yourself and the many employees of your ranch."

At least the Parker Ranch people had the satisfaction of knowing that their efforts were appreciated. Letters like these took much of the sting out of ranch reverses. And there were many other declarations of thanks from the military.

It was during these war years when another tragedy struck the Parker Ranch. Aunt Tootsie, now Mrs. Elizabeth Jane Woods, passed away in Los Angeles on April 2, 1943.

The Trust Deed of Annie Thelma Parker Smart expired with her mother's death, and on November 2, 1943, Alfred Carter turned over to Richard Smart all of the lands, personal property, livestock, and anything else comprising the Parker Ranch. On June 2 of the same year, Alfred W. Carter and A. Hartwell Carter were appointed administrators of the estate of Elizabeth Jane Woods and were discharged June 10, 1947. The estate was closed January 9, 1948.

Probably the finest tribute paid to the fabulous Aunt Tootsie is found in six paragraphs written by Richard Smart in an open letter, March 1966:

> Recently a bronze plaque has been placed in Lanakila Park in memory of my grandmother, who was John Parker III's wife and Thelma Parker's mother. She was born Elizabeth Jane Dowsett, but her Hawaiian name was Lanakila. She was one of fifteen children of Mr. and Mrs. James I. Dowsett of Honolulu, the old family home being at Palama. Her childhood nickname of "Tootsie" stayed with her throughout her life and she was known as Aunt "Tootsie" in her later years. Many of you remember her, as she lived until the middle years of World War II, but for the younger folks, I would like to reminisce a little.

Something many of you may not realize is that Lanakila Parker was a very strong and courageous young woman and had a vital influence on the destiny of Parker Ranch. As a young widow it was she who chose Alfred W. Carter to become Trustee and Ranch Manager for her little daughter Thelma's interests. We all know how important this one decision has proven.

In her late twenties she went to live with her little girl at Mana, the Parker home, and later at Puuopelu, the home of her in-laws, John Parker II and his wife Hanai. Because Kupuna Hanai only spoke Hawaiian it was necessary that my grandmother learn the language. In later life she was forever grateful for this knowledge and experience.

Although Lanakila Parker took my mother to California for her education, she never let her lose sight of her homeland. By frequent trips home she instilled a love of our land into the heart of my mother, and a generation later she did the same for me.

Long periods of my grandmother's life were shadowed by court litigation to protect the interests of Parker Ranch. She had a fighter's heart when it came to a court battle over lands, preservation of trusts, and the meeting of obligations. Her life was a full one, and she brought happiness and friendship to many, but most of all, hers was a gift of warmth for her native land, Hawaii Nei.

It is with humble pride that I have bestowed the name, Lanakila, on the little park in the center of our community. Lanakila, which means "victorious," is indeed a fitting name to remember such a noble person.

"*Me ke aloha i ho'oili pumehana ia no* Lanakila.

(Signed) Richard Smart

Although Alfred Carter was in his mid-seventies in these World War II years, and his health was precarious, the job he did—even when he was ill—was prodigious. "Age is no calendar thing," he often repeated as the birthdays piled up. In retrospect, it is a wonder that he lived so long, for he was terminally ill. He once wrote to a friend: "I am built so that I cannot get fullness out of my occupation unless I am driving at something. I do not believe that a person is ever satisfactorily occupied unless he is up against something that is hard or looks as if it were hard."

Along with his determined drive, he possessed a rare talent to convince others that they could do the same thing. One of his admiring *paniolos* once said: "When the boss says somethin', you gotta believe him; if he tells you a rooster can pull a freight train, *hoaloha* [friend], you'd better go ahead an' hitch up that rooster!"

But now with bad health suddenly dogging his footsteps, he lamented, "It is very aggravating to be laid up at a time like this."

Twenty years before this, as mentioned earlier, a horse threw him and his back was injured. The result was a constant backache. But it was not until he was in his seventies that he knew the seriousness of the injury. At this late date an X-ray examination showed that his lower vertebrae had been severely fractured. It is amazing that the continuous trouble which it gave him never slowed him down. Even a vicious attack of angina pectoris in 1936 did not slow his step. Nor did two severe operations, one in 1941 and one in 1942, stop the man in his will to go on.

Not until almost a year after the armistice was signed did the big blow strike him—malignancy. During 1946 and 1947 he had to undergo major surgery that involved long hospitalizations, the last one stretching over a year and a half. But he still fought back.

Despite the crippling effect of his illness, his indomitable will kept him at his responsibilities. He was not quite ready to let go. He continued having his faithful secretary of twenty years, Lucille Brundage, make daily bedside visits to keep him acquainted with all the important business transactions which needed his attention; and he unhesitatingly continued to assist his son Hartwell in conducting the ranch operation.

But now his health was slipping away more rapidly. The conferences with his son and secretary necessarily had to be restricted. The old gentleman said in his closing days, "Except for bad health, I don't regret growing old; I count it a privilege denied to too many."

Time finally did run out, and Alfred Wellington Carter passed away on April 27, 1949. He had lived a life that was full and complete and satisfying—and the ranch dynasty with which he had had so much to do in building was truly his monument. His own works had immortalized him.

Today the name of Alfred Wellington Carter is legendary in the history of the Parker Ranch, spoken of with reverence. He assumed the managership and trusteeship of the cattle kingdom on September 25, 1899, and remained in that capacity until he turned the reins over to his son in 1937, a span of thirty-eight years.

He had been a businessman, lawyer, cattleman, and financial genius. He and his wife, Edith Hartwell Carter, had lived a life that sparkled with success. He often said in his later years: "I've certainly known the love of a good woman."

Alfred Carter made another contribution to making Parker Ranch the thing it is today. Carter was an ardent bird lover. Nothing pleased him more, for example, than to look to the sky and watch the *nene* geese form their flight tracery; or to watch the bright cardinal, and listen to the thrush. He was one to be enchanted by the sight of seabirds dipping and fluttering along the surf line, going home. The flight of splay-tailed birds like the snow-white terns and the jet-black frigate birds thrilled him. Often he'd talk about the weird whimpering of the sandpipers as they beat the air, or about observing a snipe with its odd way of flying, darting several times in different directions before it settled down to a steady, straight course.

His efforts from the beginning had much to do with the introduction and protection of birds. As early as 1907 the legislature passed a bill to provide protection of certain birds within the Territory. This bill was actually personally drafted by Carter partly to protect perching and beneficial birds, and partly on behalf of the *nene* (Hawaiian goose and the state bird), which at the time was practically extinct.

Only a small flock of the *nene* made their home on the ranch, and only isolated flights of them were occasionally seen elsewhere on Hawaii. But promiscuous shooting throughout the Island was rapidly reducing the beautiful *nene* to the status of the dodo bird. Carter's bill no doubt saved this goose for posterity. The bird, indigenous to Hawaii, is now occasionally seen flying in graceful V-clusters over the Island. In fact, a large flock of them is currently being cultured at Pohakuloa, Hawaii, by the Territorial Board of Forestry.

Carter also imported pheasants and released them on the ranch. They did tremendously well and are a common sight today. He brought in golden-voiced Chinese thrushes, termed *wah mee*, also turning them loose on the ranch. That was in 1923, and today the thrush's voice is still heard, as is the flutelike trill of the meadowlark. As far back as 1938 Mr. George Munroe, the well-known ornithologist, contacted Alfred Carter in connection with hunters' massive destruction of shorebirds, pointing out that the Board of Agriculture viewed the matter with seeming indifference.

Carter lost no time in writing the Board and, among other things, stipulating that plover—the most numerous of Hawaiian shorebirds—were invaluable as destroyers of insects. He strongly recommended protection for these shorebirds and others and even volunteered to appear before the Board to give the facts as he had discovered them over the years.

Carter loved birds, knowing they were part of the land, the air, and the sea. He confided to a friend, "There is a mystery attached to the variety and perfection of nature—a mystery which stirs the wonder of a child, and gives a grown man or woman perspective."

12

The Ranch Now

FOR A LONG TIME during Alfred Carter's decline in health, he had been giving more and more time to indoctrinating his son, Hartwell, into the machinations of operating and managing the ranch.

Young Hartwell was appointed as official manager of the whole setup in 1937, but father and son continued working as a team in the management. Due to so many of the senior Carter's ranch innovations and methods having been introduced, the whole scheme of things almost carried on of its own momentum.

The ranch needed direction, but so many of the basic principles had already been instituted that now all they needed was constant application and supervision. Under Hartwell Carter's good management, the next twenty-three-year span found the ranch continuing to progress and prosper. Young Carter had inherited his father's talent for delegating authority. He went on delegating—and successfully.

The ranch had certainly entered into an era of ascendancy. Additional acreage had been purchased to expand the operations, and some had been sold. By 1960 Richard Smart resolved to turn his full time to ranching. Twenty-five years of theater and supperclub work had been gratifyingly successful, but now he felt the moral obligation of taking up where his people had left off. He decided to make Puuopelu his permanent home. He came to it as a forthright, observant man who had a honed sense of duty. He has since said, laughing, "I was as serious as a man with a sack of dynamite." In looking back, he now confesses that he must have had the nerve of a steeplejack to undertake the running of the ranch.

Smart appointed the capable Richard Penhallow as his manager and arranged to share managerial responsibilities with him. Penhallow had come to the ranch in 1947 from the Onomea Plantation. As for the Hawaii Meat Company which had become so integral a part of the Parker Ranch operation, Smart became the majority stockholder and was now more closely identified with its functioning.

Upon accepting the appointment as Parker Ranch manager in 1960, Penhallow already had hard and fast principles in mind with reference to the ranch's problems. He came in with full knowledge that major costs of running and maintaining a property like Parker Ranch do not decrease. Taxes, rental, purchases, wages (and fringe benefits), marketing costs, move only upward. He acknowledged, therefore, that more income must be produced to cover the costs and justify the maintenance of the investment by earning some net interest on it. He stated, "Obviously, higher and best use of the property is the only solution." He listed what he considered the opportunities for larger use as:

1. Leasing facilities for business development.
2. Developing services which a ranch can supply to item 1.
3. Producing more beef.
4. Increasing the efficiency of factors serving 3.

Working diligently along with Smart, he proceeded to institute all the principles which he believed in. By the end of two years the initial phases of Opportunity Number 1 were well underway. Smart had facilitated the plans of Waimea properties and those of Mr. Laurance Rockefeller. Exploitation of the recreational aspects of this item were soon to follow. Much progress was made—and all of it financially advantageous.

The leasing of facilities for business development had progressed tremendously. Expansion, improvement, and additional investment involved aspects of the business such as the service station, the dairy, the bank, the post office, the meat market, the grain storage, and the feed yard.

Item Number 3 continued to be the hub of all things. In seeking more business, more emphasis was put upon providing a dependable supply of graded carcasses to market, and in competing more strenuously pricewise with the imports which supplied the opposite end of the quality chain.

As for Opportunity Number 4, substantial increased efficiency stemmed from the spreading of the overhead over higher numbers of sale animals. The statistics proved this. Meanwhile, mineral and feed supplementation on pastures continued to be studied and experimented with. Nor was breed improvement by the selection of sire material from performance tests overlooked. The important well at Puako was enlarged. More irrigated fields were laid out scientifically to use the water in the most efficient way. These were just some of the strides taken to step up the efficiency and profits of the ranch.

So, by late 1962 some excellent forward steps had been promulgated by Penhallow and Smart. The duo efforts and thinking in team fashion combined to make for increased economic improvement of the ranch. Like all schemes for betterment, their plans were carefully laid out, closely watched, and resolutely carried through.

The year 1962 was also important to the Parker Ranch because a new era started with Radcliffe (Rally) Greenwell taking over the managerial duties. Owner Richard Smart designated the tall, rangy Greenwell as manager on September 27.

In the open announcement in the Parker Ranch news organ for October 1962, Smart declared: "Rally is not new to ranching. Far from it. He was born on a ranch in Kona, grew up on a ranch, and has spent his adult years on a ranch. He is the first

Parker Ranch cowboy to be named general manager. You all know Norman Brand (Parker Ranch business manager), who has been with us since 1944. He has the interest of the ranch at heart and I know he and Rally will make a fine working team. I do not contemplate any other changes at this time. I only ask that you give Rally the wholehearted cooperation that you have given Dick Penhallow. I am sure you will."

It happened that tall, genial Greenwell was a member of one of the Big Island's oldest ranching families. He was born on December 25, 1914, at Kona, son of Mr. and Mrs. Frank R. Greenwell. He had joined the Parker Ranch in 1934 at the age of twenty. Working as a *paniolo*, he rose to the position of foreman.

Greenwell's talents were recognized by the late Ronald Von Holt, then manager of Kahua Ranch. Von Holt promoted him to the job of assistant manager, a post he held until January 1, 1956, when he returned to Parker Ranch as foreman of Paauhau area under manager Hartwell Carter. Upon Hartwell Carter's retirement in 1960, Greenwell was moved up to administrative assistant. His superior work and responsible administration continued to pay off, and in 1961 he was named assistant manager.

Immediately upon taking over the reins, Greenwell asked through the ranch's monthly *Paka Paniolo* for the help and assistance of all employees. He said: "These are the two things that I need—your fullest cooperation and deepest aloha. I have been on this ranch over half of my life. I feel it gives me greater understanding of all our problems."

His declaration sprang from deep humility and friendliness. He knew he could acquit himself creditably only if he had the unreserved help of those under him. He knew he faced a man-killing job.

Greenwell, a realist, recognized that many of the employees would be harboring thoughts about who might be released from service and who might be transferred to duties different from those that they had been performing. He quickly allayed most doubts and fears by explaining, "I know you are all wondering just what changes management does contemplate. They are not many. But what changes have been made and will be made in the future, let me assure you that they are with the welfare of the ranch and the ranch families at heart."

Instead of outlining personnel changes, he pointed out changes which he planned to make in operation and procedure. They related mostly to moving herds to more suitable areas, the rebuilding of stables at Makahalau, and several other operational changes. But he made it emphatic that "There is to be no change on the stations at this time."

He erased any further doubts about personnel ruptures and turmoil when he added, "I plan to meet some of the key foremen every morning to discuss ranch problems with them and with anyone else who wishes to see me. I want each Parker Ranch employee to feel free to come to me and discuss his problems. It is with deep humility that I accept this position. No one knows better than I that, without your help—every man and woman on Parker Ranch—I cannot do the job that I have set for myself."

Greenwell went to work at once with his *paniolos* and, in his low-modulated voice, began giving the orders in the tongue which the men best liked and understood. He remembered the days when all ranch orders were issued in the Hawaiian language. There is a spill-over from the early years, and today the talk on the range is still salted with many Hawaiian words and expressions. To a *malihini* (newcomer) much of it is incomprehensible, but it lends a soft, melodic tone to their speech and is reminiscent of friendly, early Hawaiian days when the mother language softened and colored communication.

Greenwell knew of the great cattle drives made at night in order to take advantage of the cooler weather conditions and the crossing of highways when there was a minimum of oncoming traffic. He remembered when the herds were swum out to waiting boats off Kawaihae on the northwest coast.

Changes, innovations, and experiments have always been part of the code of operation at Parker Ranch. Ranch Manager Greenwell and Richard Smart were constantly alert for anything new which promised improvement. Their consultations, for example, came up with a drastic change which was reported from Kamuela on February 9, 1963. It involved the phasing out of the sheep station on Humuula's 42,000 acres, which had run as many as 30,000 sheep since it had been acquired by the ranch in 1914. Originally it had been about 4,500 head. The move proved a gainful one.

For many years thousands of Parker Ranch cattle have been barged from the Big Island to Oahu, where they are turned into the Hawaii Meat Company's feedlots at Campbell Industrial Park. Some thirty Island ranchers are involved in the ownership of the Hawaii Meat Company, which began business in 1909, and it is fortunate that the firm has this kind of financial backing, for in 1967 it was able to complete its $1,000,000 feedlot and its $700,000 feedmill. Figuratively speaking, Richard Smart has been giving the new setup a standing ovation. Why? Simply because his cattle are now being custom fed—electronically.

The Hawaii Meat Company's new modernization takes Parker Ranch calves six to eight months after their weaning, puts them in feedlots for 150 to 175 days of pampering and pen-feeding. The contented animals gain weight maximally. Or, as Richard Smart points out, "We put them on this high-energy food for five or six months. It normally puts three pounds of meat on them per day, but it takes seven pounds of this food to add a pound of beef. It's expensive—but it works!"

Eighty percent of the feed is imported to Hawaii; the only locally grown product is a comparatively expensive pineapple bran. The feed from the mainland is shipped in 23-ton containers and hauled from the harbor to the Hawaii Meat Company in truck trailers. The container cargoes are stationed over a floor grating and sluiced to one of the four 1,000-ton storage tanks or to a 4,000-ton warehouse. From there, as needed, quantities of it are transferred to the holding bins. Some of the items like barley and wheat have to first be subjected to special treatment. There is a process of sifting out impurities in a massive, electrically operated scalper. Then the grains are made more readily digestible by means of rolling and steaming.

The heart of the whole process is found in a 13-by-2-foot electronic feedmill control room where an electronic brain occupies one wall. The multitude of dials, correctly regulated, spell out the answers to what is the best possible combination of feeds at the lowest possible price. This "nutrient cost factor" comes from a computer at one of the West Coast universities. The Hawaii Meat Company decided to purchase the wanted information in lieu of buying a computer that would cost about a quarter of a million dollars.

When the mainland computer is fed some 150 possible cattle feeds, it digests all the data and responds with the most economical balanced cattle diet, or "menu," for a given two- to three-week period. The information is programmed onto cartridges and, in turn, relayed electronically to the various holding bins. One cartridge "orders" the exact amount of alfalfa, wheat, corn, rolled barley, or other grains. A second cartridge orders the mineral preparation. Immediately, the ordered products are delivered to a mammoth overhead auger-scale. In short order, a nutritious combination of feed is mixed and trucked to the feeding pens.

Electronics continue to have a big hand in this. For example, push-button control dumps the feed into a delivery truck, and the cargo is automatically ejected into the individual feeding bins. The truck driver distributes the correct and exact rations to the right pens, and records are notated on a computer punch-card.

True, custom-fed cattle obviously cost the rancher more than those raised on range grass, but he frees his valuable grazing land for additional cattle production. Basically, ranch income actually increases when a rancher doubles his production with increased cow herds. At this writing, the Parker Ranch and many other cattle ranches, have found it an advantage to pen-feed calves at twelve to eighteen months of age. As for usage of the electrical installations for selecting and distributing the proper feed—that is an advantage in itself.

A small feedlot operation was put under way right on the ranch. In March 1969 an experimental feedlot was initiated at Holoholoku, and hopes rode high at its installation. Much thought and study had gone into the plans, and it shaped up as a foolproof operation.

Two lots of 100 head each were to be fed out to market finish. Ordinarily, as pointed out, the feeder cattle were barged to Oahu to the feedlot for finishing and marketing, so this new arrangement represented a radical departure. In lieu of the other program, now the ranch was experimenting with finishing cattle on homegrown corn silage. On Oahu the animals had been finished on rations formulated with combinations of grains imported from out of the Islands. Cost and tangible results would naturally be the determining factors in this new mode of fattening Parker Ranch cattle.

An experienced grain farmer from Iowa, Mr. Wallace Coleman, had ventured into the planting of grain crops on the Big Island, and he selected the Waikii area for the reason that it was close, plus the fact that in the past the ranch had already successfully grown hundreds of acres of fine corn there. At least there was no risk about the soil and climate being unsatisfactory. Good silage for the Parker Ranch was assured. Time alone would prove or disprove the wisdom of the move.

A business of the Parker Ranch's proportions and dimensions has to be subject to change, and every year management continues to "play it by ear." Experimentation in air-freighting cattle from Hawaii to California began in June 1970. A sample shipment had been made as early as March of that year, but five jet shipments (500,000 pounds or about 1,100 head) were made during the week beginning June 8. The event was a history-making 3,000-mile "cattle drive" from Waimea to Bakersfield, California, and promised to hold some key answers for the future of the Big Island ranching businesses.

That week's flight of animals was not for immediate conversion to meat, but involved a direct sale to an independent ranch owner. It was, however, a test for further flights to Oakland, California, thence by truck to feedlots at Bakersfield, 300 miles to the south. It all began with a traditional roundup of feeder cattle from the grassy South Kohala rangeland, then a trucking job to Hilo, where the animals were put aboard giant Trans-International Airlines (TIA) DC-8's. This was a massive experiment to take advantage of cheaper feed on the mainland, plus substitution of a five-hour airflight for the usual seventeen-hour barge trip from Kawaihae to Honolulu. Cutting down on the hours of weight-affecting stress to the animals was an important item, but the more important economic benefit was in getting the cattle to the cheaper feed grain, rather than paying $30 per ton to bring the feed to Hawaii—a state which grows but a minimal amount of grain at all.

The problem was well summed up when Parker Ranch business manager Robert Eastman said, "It takes seven pounds of feed to put one pound on an animal, and we have to ship all our grain in from the mainland at very high prices. Since feed is cheaper over there, that may be the place to fatten them up for market." Like so many other things, this would be worked out by time and experimentation.

Despite all the drastic changes in ranch operation over the years, one basic phase of it has been only minimally altered; and that is the *paniolos'* actual handling of the stock. It has been speeded up and sharpened, but basically its sameness is there.

Watching a Parker Ranch cattle operation today is a lesson in assembly-line technique. It is hard, dusty, sweaty work, but the highly trained *paniolos* go at their chores with gusto and dedication. Watching a herd of five-month-old calves assembled at a Waikii paddock, you know that you are witnessing talented cowboys doing the thing they know and do best.

The bawling calves are fed in a steady stream to highly specialized paddock crews. These four operations are performed at a rate of three animals a minute.

(1) Each animal is imprinted with two brands—the well-known Parker *P* is implanted, and a numeral indicating the year of birth is scorched in.

(2) Each animal is administered two shots—one an inoculation against blackleg, and the other for pinkeye. If any calf shows a trace of the latter, a lotion of mixed bacterin is splashed into its eyes.

(3) Ears are notched for identification; that is, they are cropped twice—one ear with a flat edge and the other with a *V*-nick—all for quick identification in the brush.

(4) The animals are dehorned, and the young bulls are desexed. What look like jumbo fingernail clippers are used in snipping off the horns, then the stumps are painted with an antiseptic coagulent to prevent bleeding and infection. The desexing is done just as quickly and painlessly. Here, too, the wound is immediately antisepticized to preclude infection and bleeding.

The herding, chuting, and roping throughout all this operation is done with great dexterity. The finely trained horses contribute a splendid dimension to the whole process. Calves bawl for their mothers. *Paniolos* work in an open pen, some on horseback, pushing, shoving with their mounts; some roping. The "ground crew" wrestles roped calves, some castrating, some inoculating, some wielding branding irons. Calves are lassoed by their hind legs, jerked up sharply, and trip and fall. One iron brands the animal's age, one marks the ranch's letter, high on the rump for the number, low on the thigh for the *P*.

Discussion here is of cattle born of the regular Parker Ranch herds. But in this modern era, another vintage of cattle is sometimes reckoned with—wild cattle that range the far, unfenced, unpatrolled reaches of northern Hawaii and are seldom sighted by man.

The ruggedness and wildness of some areas of Parker Ranch terrain even today offer refuge for cattle which must occasionally be rounded up and brought in. These are rogue animals, extremely fierce when cornered.

When sufficient Parker Ranch wild cattle are seen and reported in far reaches of the ranch, a "posse" is made up and sets out to capture and bring in the wild ones. Not long ago a roundup of this kind was reported in the ranch's monthly paper, *Paka Paniolo*, and it makes for interesting reading to those who think all ranches have domesticated animals safely and securely fenced in in paddocks or bounded rangelands:

"Recently our Kohala cowboys were joined by Rally Greenwell and the Waimea cowboys on a wild cattle drive in rugged Honokane over in Kohala. Led by the Kohala *kamaainas*, the men drove the huge paddock on foot, the terrain being too swampy, rough and tangled to be practical to drive on horseback. Thirty wild cattle were rounded up and corralled. One bull was lost when he cleared the corral fence and went back into the deep forest.

"Among the thirty head captured was an old steer which had been seen many times but which had always eluded his captors. He is reported to be over fifteen years old. This job, though very dangerous, was like a shot in the arm to the old-timers who recounted their experience with much excitement at the end of the day's work. The real rugged old days of cowpunching wild cattle are seldom experienced these days and the men regard it as somewhat of a treat and a challenge to outsmart and outmaneuver an *'ahiu.'* "

From time to time over the years, severe droughts have descended upon the Parker Ranch region, threatening man, flora, and fauna. One never knows when the vicious natural disaster cycles will hit. Too often when the troubles come in the cattle-raising business, they come as drought, flood, or fire.

On September 15, 1965, a meeting of the ranch's top hands concerned itself with what to do about the current drastic water shortage. Drought had struck the range for many months. It was described as a worse drought than the one of 1962, which cost the ranch much money and brought on much herd hardship.

Particularly, the Kohala watershed had failed in its supply. That area ordinarily furnished a bountiful water supply to Hamakua, Waimea, Puako, and Kawaihae. This time it was less than niggardly. The situation was extremely acute, and ranch manager Rally Greenwell pleaded with everyone to cooperate and conserve water in every possible way, making suggestions as to how they could do their part.

Officer manager Brand advised that some hope lay in the Department of Land and Natural Resources' approval to go ahead with connecting the ranch's four-inch pipeline across the Kamuela Airport access road in order to pump water from the Puuopelu Reservoir up to Holoholoku. This promised to alleviate the problem somewhat. Any kind of relief, large or small, was needed. Even the limited water holes in the Keanakolu region began to look like a last resort, and plans were made to move the thirsty herds farther toward the mountains.

At the end of the meeting the top hands, led by Greenwell, began a field inspection of the Alakahi water intake. Evidence of stark drought faced them all along the route. At the intake a small trickle of water no wider than ten or twelve inches and about a half inch deep rolled over the stones into the intake dam. The water level at the intake was below the four-inch pipeline which ordinarily transports the water down the mountain to where it is needed. The lower side of the dam showed the ditch to be dry.

Descending from the high levels, the party inspected the three county reservoirs—Waimea's domestic water supply— which receive their gallonage through the *puka puka* pipe which the people of Waimea had begged the government to replace. Of the three reservoirs, two were totally dry, and the last one only partially filled. It was more obvious than ever that, unless something tangible could be done soon about developing the watershed things would go from bad to worse.

Sporadic droughts such as this have hampered Hawaiian ranching over the decades. This one finally ended, of course, in torrents of rain. But the Parker Ranch's history has been studded with instances where rainfall was the one thought occupying everyone's mind over long periods of time.

Rainfall, or lack of it, has even worked its way into some of the legends of the Island. Old *meles* of the Hawaiians touch upon the subject. The Parker Ranch, like all of Hawaii, is rife with legends. One of the colorful ones which is handed down from year to year in connection with this vast region and its reliance on water, is the one about the Rain Rock. The old Hawaiians called it *"Manaua,"* the Rain Rock god. This particular boulder on the property had for generations been worshiped by the Polynesians as one of the legendary and important gods.

When Richard Smart leased out some of his Parker property for resort use, he made it a point that the Rain Rock would not be part of the deal or be disturbed in any way, specifying this condition in the lease. To ensure that the conditions be observed to the letter, and to please the old Hawaiians, Smart even had a low fence built around the rock.

Shortly afterward, there was a severe drought. Rainless skies and torrid weather held sway until springs and wells dried up totally. The hills, slopes, and valleys became dehydrated, and the grass and foliage shrank and died. Even aged Hawaiians could not remember having seen so severe a drought. The young and old brought offerings of flowers and *maile* to the Rain Rock to appease the god. But there was still no sign of precipitation; nor was there any promise of it in the near future. Finally, in desperation the Hawaiians insisted that the Rain Rock god was probably angered at being hemmed in by a fence.

Richard Smart was away from the ranch at the time, but some of his men saw to it that the gate to the fence enclosure was left ajar; this presumably would give the god some measure of freedom. But the drought continued. An eerie silence permeated the parched Hawaiian hills and valleys. Even massive Mauna Kea glowered down upon the lowlands with an austerity that was lava-dry and forbidding. Days of blazing sun sucked the life out of grass, vine, and tree. The herds stood numbly, not knowing where to go to slake their thirst. All over the land was a sense of something waiting, waiting. At this time Richard Smart returned from the mainland and immediately had the fence taken down.

The very night of the fence removal, huge masses of cumulus clouds began to gather. A rising wind began to bring a promise of storm, and then rain fell in the nearby Kohala Mountain region. The Hawaiians reasoned that the rain gods of that area had been sympathetic with Manaua of this area, and were demonstrating their approval of his release. Shortly thereafter, lightning flickered across the mountains. The cattle began moving slowly in the direction of the muttering heights. Suddenly the skies thundered like the slamming of a thousand barn doors, and precious rains descended upon the Parker Ranch's huge acreage in life-giving quantities. All was well again now that Manaua had been placated.

In times past, the winter rains too often drained off the lands in creeks and streams and found their way to the sea. But now bulldozers scrape out wide and deep areas which have the capacity to store up millions of gallons of water to tide over the arid spells. The bulldozing is done during the dry period. Then, after the first rainfall, the cattle are driven into the dug-out basins to trample the earth into a hard base. Sometimes this is even done again after a second rain to ensure a solid, almost watertight bottom where the moisture loss will be minimal.

Another great change which has taken place down through the years under a chain of able managers involves the paddocks. Their efficiency has wrought vast differences in the way the herds were once handled. In the years before, the cattle roamed at will, becoming wild and scraggy, tough as a beef item. They traveled far for good range, and farther for water. With today's paddocks, fresh water is supplied in a simple way. There are over 150 paddocks that measure in size from a few acres well into the hundreds. They are so important that they are even dignified with names. Christmas Paddock, for example, was completed on December 25. Rain Paddock was constructed during drenching Kamuela downpours. As for fencing, literally hundreds of miles are involved—and all without use of barbed wire.

The tragedies of forest and brush fire over the years have been sporadic and often devastating. Old-timers still talk of the famous Hanaipoe fire of 1918, which started in Umikoa and burned all the way to Hanaipoe, burning for about six months. It was an unbelievably stubborn conflagration, and men had to be pulled from their ranch jobs to bring the persistent flames under control.

The largest brush and grass fire in Hawaii's recorded history struck much of the Parker Ranch area in 1969. September had been bright, yellow, glaring, and the heat was unbearable. Then someone put a match to the tinder-dry grass. The fire started burning out of control on September 27 near the Puuanahulu Village in the North Kona. It forced the closing of Mamalahoa Highway between Waimea and Kailua-Kona, and with strong winds whipping the leaping flames, hundreds of already parched acres of grass and bush were burned. Then the conflagration jumped the road in the Parker and Puuwaawaa Ranch land region and roared on, still totally out of control.

Fire-fighting equipment from Captain Cook, Honokaa, Waimea, and Hilo moved into the area. Bulldozers began cutting fire lanes. Homes and livestock appeared to be safe at first, but wild sheep, goats, and pigs were trapped in the holocaust. It burned and seethed, spilling in every direction despite the efforts of trained fire fighters and raw recruits.

By October 1, 37,000 acres had been burned over. The State Division of Forestry arranged for water-laden crop dusters to fly and "bomb" the hotter spots in the fire. Bulldozed firebreaks and a series of natural lava walls were containing some of the blazing

fronts, but the problem was still a lethal one. All available manpower was still being utilized, but progress seemed nil.

Some sixty men fought the more raging front, and they
included Parker Ranch employees, Hawaii County firemen, and
Division of Forestry employees. They fought the battle with
over thirty pieces of ground equipment and a helicopter, which
proved particularly important in ferrying men from spot to
spot, and in bringing in equipment, water, meals, and first-aid
supplies.

By October 3 the flames formed a fourteen-mile front and
had burned over 39,000 acres. The main road (Highway 19) from
Kailua-Kona to Waimea and Hilo had been jumped and left far
behind. Forty *paniolos* from Parker Ranch made up part of the
fighting force, requiring many hours of overtime and extra
shifts. Every day was one of heavy, insufferable heat.

The week-old fire was abetted by 45-mile-an-hour winds
blustering through brush and trees. The roaring flames covered
the area *mauka* toward Puuwaawaa Ranch to the east and
gnawed hungrily upward to the slopes of Hualalai. The northern perimeter toward Waimea was totally blackened. With leaping fire still advancing, some 200 to 300 smoldering areas remained and required continual surveillance. The Hawaii
County Fire Department, ably directed by battalion chief Alex
Von Arnswaldt, announced that the fires were finally contained
between two lava flows and a network of bulldozed firebreaks.
By that time over eighty men were working full time in the fiery
region.

Fortunately, no livestock was lost, but some of the finest
stands of native trees and plants, such as *obia, mamani, lama,* and
kauwila trees were destroyed. Wardens admitted that much wild
game in the region had suffered heavy causaulties. The fire
located between the 1859 and 1801 lava flows caused considerable
damage to utility poles and fence posts. Much range grass, of
course, was completely wiped out. Places that, earlier in the
year, had been green, were left black and charred.

Only by dedicated, courageous fire fighting had the flames been checked, and many cattle, homes, and buildings not destroyed. A system of firebreaks by bulldozers kept the raging inferno from spreading to the best grazing land on Parker Ranch. Over twenty miles of firebreaks had been bulldozed, and old-timers remarked that never had so many bulldozers and pieces of heavy equipment been seen at any one time in the West Hawaii area.

With the fire's final containment a few days later, the cause of the conflagration was still unknown, but there was valid reason to believe that arson was at the root of it. Brush and grass fires continued to plague the ranch and adjacent properties into the early winter months. In late October another 4,000-acre fire broke loose on Kahua Ranch and Hawaiian Homes Commission lands. At three of the fires proof of arson was unmistakable.

13

Today's Kamuela

and Puuopelu

K A M U E L A (meaning Samuel) has been mentioned so many times in this account that it is now necessary to furnish a capsule picture of it as it is today. Kamuela and Waimea are really one and the same thing; the former is the official postal designation for the latter. The names are interchangeable.

Kamuela, or Waimea, is a village modeled after a *paniolo's* needs. This accounts for the general store where *paniolos* and their families can purchase needed supplies and merchandise. There is a big ranch restaurant, and many houses built for the families of the various hands. With the advent of the automobile and truck, garages and gas stations sprang up. Christian churches and Buddhist temples have firmly taken root.

But something new has crept in with recent "modernization" (in quotes because Richard Smart's architectural leaning for the Kamuela is toward the Victorian, or the style of the Monarchy period which held sway during the days of Samuel Parker). So, Smart has seen to it that the new ranch office, bank, and post office have been built with this style predominating. An excellent auditorium and theater have been remodeled, and they, too, reflect his architectural taste. The complex is called the "Kahilu" in honor of Richard Smart's mother—using only the first three syllables of her long Hawaiian name. Bright red and white trim characterize the "Kahilu," and the flavor of royalty is maintained.

Puuopelu, the current family home at Kamuela, is situated almost in the middle of today's huge Parker Ranch. John Parker II had started the main portion of the rambling ranchhouse-type structure in 1863, but in the late 1860s he improved it and increased it in size. *Puuopelu* is Hawaiian for "Hill of Hiding." Literally, *puu* means "hill," and *pelu* means "doubled up." It is said to be named after a princess who sought refuge during an ancient Polynesian battle. Every room of the century-old structure is rich with lore and legend of yesteryear.

As you enter its double hall doors, the first thing which catches the eye is a huge rock-crystal chandelier. Beyond the entrance hall is a large, high-ceilinged living room, where a large antique Portuguese table catches the attention. Renoir graces one wall. Along the solidly mirrored wall to the right are glass shelves containing some fifty shining koa calabashes, whispering of old Hawaii. It would be heresy to pass by this rare collection with hurried steps. There is a wide, handsome fireplace, and above its mantel is a wide, antique Austrian mirror reflecting the splendor of the room.

The library is directly ahead, and to the left the dining room —gracious and suggestive of unstinted hospitality. The portraits on the wall are of Richard Smart's mother, Thelma Kahiluonapuaapiilani Parker Smart, and one of his grandmother, the now legendary Elizabeth Jane Lanakila Dowsett Parker. Both likenesses have much in common, with finely chiseled classic faces. These two women bequeathed a vast and rich ranch to Richard Smart, and he is managing and developing it into an even better thing for those who have remained loyal to the heritage which they left. Looking up at them, one realizes that he is carrying out the plan for the "ranch family" begun by them.

All the rooms are spacious and contain collections of items of eye-catching interest. There are other pictures that arrest your attention, furniture that invites lingering study. The house has five bedrooms, each furnished with an enormous four-poster bed, hand-carved from koa wood. Beautiful Hawaiian quilts cover them, and they seem to speak softly of people born and people deceased. Here is a distinct mixture of American, European, and Asian influence.

A loyal staff of five maintains the spotlessness of this sprawling white house, to say nothing of the neatly manicured lawns, hedges, and plants. Puuopelu befits its owner, who makes it his home year in and year out.

Ambitious planning has always characterized the Parker Ranch. Every major move is carefully thought out, assessed, and weighed. And much of the success of the enterprise is attributable to Richard Smart's willingness to listen to experts on ranching matters. It has made for a fine and solid *esprit de corps*. In November 1964, interviewed by the Sunday editor of the Honolulu *Advertiser*, A. E. P. Wall, Smart said: "I have a very fine manager. One of the best cattlemen in the State—Radcliffe Greenwell. My business manager is Norman Brand. I usually get together with Rally and Norman in the morning and we have a three-way conference. I concern myself mainly with land matters and certain top questions of policy. You might also call me a sort of trouble shooter for certain personnel problems, especially regarding land and housing. The cattle aspect of the ranch is absolutely in Rally's hands."

There is a constant and perpetual receptiveness to new ideas which might serve as the germ or embryo for experimentation and further development. It keeps the whole enterprise flexible and fluid. As for additional changes, Smart pointed out that the ranch had changed to a cow-calf operation to meet the local demand for government-inspected beef. He made it clear that the reason for this was due to such an influx of scores of thousands of housewives from the mainland to the Islands.

When Mr. Wall wanted to know what was meant by "cow-calf" operation, Smart explained: "The cattle leave the ranch at a much lighter weight than before, and are sent to Ewa on Oahu where they are fed for about 140 days before they go to market. The feeders come off the ranch when they weigh about 600 pounds. They may be anywhere between 16 and 22 months old, with the average about 20 months. They stay at the feed lot until they reach about 1,000 pounds. The Hawaii Meat Company feed lot at Ewa is operated, under a managerial contract, by Diamond A Ranch. There we have the benefit of scientific experiments that are going on all the time to try to improve the feed formula."

He explained that when the time comes for slaughtering, the cattle are taken over by the Hawaii Meat Company, and pointed out that he is one of about thirty ranchers from all Islands who own stock in Hawaii Meat, which handles the marketing.

He went on: "We are able to market all we can produce, even though about 30 percent of our market has been taken by foreign imports—compared to 11 percent on the Mainland. We also compete with meat brought in from the Mainland, but we feel we have better beef to sell.

"We can compete easily with the Mainland, but it is hard to compete with foreign countries that pay lower wages, have lower expenses in general and ship in lower grades of beef. Two advantages we have over Mainland beef is that we do not have to chill ours, and we can provide quick delivery after an order is placed."

When asked about other changes, Smart was quick to point out several of the new things which influenced the business—the mechanization now resorted to, the more efficient accounting recently installed, the many shortcuts taken in business administration—all maneuvers meaning, among other things, a cutting away of red tape to get things done.

In addition, there had been much streamlining of the staff, much increasing of pipelines and new pumps, which lessened the man hours formerly required. Shipping the cattle from the range to Kawaihae by truck in lieu of herding them via cow-hands, had been an economic and time-saving step.

As for personnel management, today ranch hands are on a forty-hour-a-week basis. "Our ranch hands," Smart explained, "are a wonderful bunch of people. If they see something that needs to be done, they simply do it without being asked." He continued: "The people who get into the better ranch jobs in the future are going to have to have an education. We have several college graduates now. We also have some men with very little education who have special ranch instincts that seem to be acquired only by experience. We have had men with more than fifty years of service, and many of our employees are second, third and fourth generation Parker Ranch people."

The ranch makes quite a thing of raising its own horses for the *paniolo* needs. But it doesn't stop at that, for Smart is also raising thoroughbreds which he sells. The luxurious Mauna Kea Hotel is stocked with his thoroughbred riding horses.

Parker Ranch is a successful business operation—and Richard Smart works at it; he lives it and breathes it. He can ride with some of the best of his *paniolos*; and he can talk knowledgeably about Renoir, Corot, El Greco, or Guardi.

His two sons, Gaillard and Antony, have little yearning to be cattlemen. Both discovered early that cattle ranching was not for them. Like all of us, they have their own concept of success, and they want theirs in their own way. They've chosen fields totally divorced from that of their father's, and he respects their independent judgment and right of choice.

So, as of the date of this writing, it seems that the current Parker Ranch dynasty is not apt to be a case of son stepping into father's shoes to keep the kingdom intact and perpetuate it.

Today the Parker Ranch constitutes a huge portion of the northwest section of the Island of Hawaii. With all its changes, its perimeter still starts on the west coast of South Kohala at Kawaihae and climbs for forty miles up the slope of Mauna Kea, the highest mountain in the Pacific, to an elevation of 7,500 feet, thus including a variety of climates and agricultural conditions. The trade winds blow in from the sea, sweep up this vast stretch of terrain, and there is abundant rain most of the time. There is neither real summer nor real winter on the ranch. The cattle range abroad throughout the year and graze on grasses that never cease to grow.

Having applied dedicated and scientific administration to the ranch over the years, during and since the Alfred Carter era, the ranch has become a showplace and demonstration plant to cattle raisers from all over the world.

14

Cattleman and Socialite

RECENT YEARS on the Parker Ranch have rivaled those fabulous days of the Samuel Parker era in social brilliance. There are fiestas, rodeos, barbecues, and assorted celebrations. Richard Smart's twenty-five years of theater and supperclub experience have contributed much to today's Parker Ranch hosting.

Having decided upon a stage career while still at Stanford University, he spent two years working with the Pasadena Community Playhouse in California, studying the profession and sharpening his talent. Smart wanted to try his wings in the theatrical world in a professional way, to succeed on the strength of his theatrical ability, and not because of his status as the sole heir to a cattle and land fortune.

So, seeking to make a name for himself, he worked steadfastly for years at his art, and improved progressively. He appeared in stage and radio plays, musical comedies, and nightclub revues throughout the United States and Europe. His singing took him to the Continent, where he played such clubs as Le Tabarin and La Ginguette in Casablanca, Le Club in Meknes, Le Roi De La Dierre in Oran, Le Fantasio in Algiers, and Le Caveau in Tunis. In the United States he played the Mocambo in Hollywood, the Versailles in New York, the Drake in Chicago, the Raddison in Minneapolis, the Five O'Clock Club in Miami Beach, and the Mayflower in Washington.

Smart was box office by the time he appeared in the Cole Porter–Moss Hart musical comedy, *Jubilee*, which opened in St. Louis in 1945. In 1947 he played the leading role opposite Nanette Fabray in the New York musical comedy *Bloomer Girl*. He starred in many other theatrical productions, appearing opposite Carol Channing in *Wonderful Town*, and with both Denise Darcel and Hildegarde in *Can Can*. He appeared in such memorable productions as *Call Me Madam, Gentlemen Prefer Blondes, Silk Stockings, One Touch of Venus, The Great Waltz, Where's Charley, The Merry Widow, Sunny, The Cat and the Fiddle, After the Ball, The Red Mill*, and others.

Despite the fact that he had an excellent baritone voice, he aspired not at all to grand opera. His preference was for the works of Gershwin, Porter, and Kern.

Richard Smart came back to Hawaii with the Straw Hat Players of San Francisco in 1948, and *49th State Revue* was put on in Honolulu. The Straw Hatters had caught on in San Francisco, where they were featured at the Golden Gate Theater. Later they played in the Mural Room of the Hotel St. Francis. Even as late as 1959 he was giving performances at the Monarch Room of the Royal Hawaiian Hotel in Waikiki.

The theater had been a soul-satisfying experience for Smart, but now there was this other inner urge tugging at him—an obligation to the ranch which had been left to him. He had to become more a part of it. He made his move back to the land and the people he called "family."

Having returned to Puuopelu, he said, "My primary interest is this ranch and what it means to Hawaii. When my mother was only eighteen, she created a trust, with the income divided three ways—my grandmother, myself and the employees of the ranch. Some of these employees are the children and the grandchildren of former employees. I have an obligation to keep the ranch intact."

He has been doing just that ever since. Today the ranch is

his life. He forfeited the boards and the lights for the people to whom he felt most indebted. He turned cattleman. But Richard Smart was not apt to turn cattleman recluse when he came home to the ranch. To the contrary, he hosted lavish social gatherings on his vast spread when time would allow.

Years have come and gone and many old, loved faces have passed from the scene. Many belonged to the workaday world of the ranch; many to the fantastic social whirl which has given Mana its aura of court royalty. Over the years the gala parties themselves would have been sufficient to put Mana on Hawaii's social map. But, with the growth of the ranch and the increasing number of Richard Smart's friends, Mana could no longer begin to accommodate the lavish entertaining. A ballroom was built in Kamuela which could accommodate well over a thousand guests. It is named Kahilu Hall after Smart's mother's Hawaiian name.

In January 1962 special airline flights brought guests to the Parker Ranch's 125th anniversary celebration. More than a thousand Islanders and mainland friends of Smart's were invited to the Holoku Ball on that Saturday. It was the highlight of a three-day celebration. Governor Quinn joined Smart in the receiving line.

The event was a carnival, circus, rodeo, sing-along, dance, picnic, musicale, and church meeting all rolled into one. But it was the diamond-studded, silk-lined, *maile*-draped Grand Holoku Ball which garnered most of the headlines. Society reporter "Steve" Wilcox of the Honolulu *Advertiser* caught the magic and fire of the ball in her column, "Party Line."

"Swashbuckling Col. Sam Parker . . . 'Lord of Mana' who ruled over the vast acreage of Parker Ranch in the late 1900s, who lit his cigars with $5.00 bills . . . and developed a legendary reputation for hospitality the world over . . . must have smiled across the years over the weekend.

"With beautiful, richly-gowned women, their handsome, urbane escorts, much music, gaiety and good food . . . and camaraderie and the reminiscences from old-timers. . . . Richard Smart present owner of Parker Ranch, celebrated its 125th anniversary with a house party climaxed by a lively Holoku Ball, which fitted easily into the tradition of his famous forefather.

"In the old days it was '*okolehao* good-time kind party' . . . this one was a 'champagne good-time kind' . . . but after upwards of a century, the emphasis at Parker Ranch clearly remains on giving the guests a good time.

"Only an hour's plane ride from Honolulu brought Oahuans up to the cool, damp plain of Waimea to meet with Hawaii guests who'd driven by car from waypoints around the Big Island. Gorgeous holokus were carefully carried in boxes and garment bags . . . all to the same purpose of being pretty-at-a-party . . . an aim that sent the young ladies of Parker Ranch in an earlier day flying across the landscape on horseback to neighboring social events with their lovely dresses wrapped in oilskin and tied to their saddle.

"The town of Kamuela, which Richard Smart has renovated in a stylized version of the Kalakaua period . . . 'cheerful and colorful,' say the advocates . . . 'gingerbready and unauthentic,' say opponents . . . is refreshingly cool.

"The gardens bloom with violets and pansies, fuschias, daisies, tremendous hydrangeas . . . thick honeysuckle, false lehua . . . the meadowy grass is thick and green . . . the air is damp . . . trees are pine and eucalyptus . . . not the swaying coconuts of the warmer lowland.

"No wonder this was a favorite 19th Century holiday retreat for royalty from Honolulu . . . even though they traveled by schooner at the mercy of a breeze . . . or overnight on the steamers . . . to be met by canoe at Kawaiahae. Ready always for a party, they'd begin at the Parker home there before driving upland by carriage or on horseback the 18 miles to Kamuela and then the further distance *mauka* to 'Mana' where the Parkers' huge ranch home sprawled.

"When they finally arrived, the *ahaainas* for as many as 1,000 lasted a week, house parties for sometimes a month or more. There were masses of flowers, the *imus* were always going, no effort was spared.

"There's always been a mingling of Island and faraway guests at ranch activities. When Hawaii was a coaling station for the ship routes of the world, handsome German, British and French naval officers spread word of 'Mana's' lavish hospitality and returned to enjoy it again.

"Kings and queens would arrive for the galas with their retinues . . . island women looking forward to the parties would have their dresses ordered months ahead from London and Paris. It was sumptuous, elegant, merry as Kalakaua . . . Waimea's part in Hawaii's Golden Age.

"This modern party lasted three days and our guess is that the countryside of Waimea lies exhausted this morning. Not only Richard's own ranch home, Puuopelu, and his guest houses . . . but seemingly every home in Kamuela was billeting guests for the big occasion.

"As well . . . summer homes along the coast line were opened by Honolulans to accommodate the overflow. Mrs. Julia Brown went up from town to have as her guests the Kenneth Browns, Samuel G. Wights, Chris Cusack.

"Friday there was a ceremonial trek back up to 'Mana' . . . no longer the hub of ranch social life but now a quiet retreat filled with memories where a museum of mementoes and the family cemetery are located. A program of massed choirs was scheduled Friday evening.

"Saturday morning the ranch appealed to guests through its time-honored lure, their love of horses . . . with a top horse show and colorful parade. Jeans on the women replaced divided skirts of yesteryear but the hats with fresh flower leis and the fun remained the same.

". . . ranch people had gone to the mountains to gather greens to decorate Kahilu, the hall named after Sam Parker's granddaughter who was Richard's mother, Thelma

Kahiluonapuaapilani. And there the Ball was held Saturday night.

"The porch was outlined in bright lights to welcome guests . . . lehus sprayed white and bright with red blossoms framed the entrance. Indoors a huge portrait of the lovely Thelma Parker was gracefully draped in crown flower and *maile* leis.

"Ferns were everywhere . . . giant tree ferns against the wall, lehua in natural green wired with red flowers, baskets of *kupukupu* fern hung from the ceiling, garlands of fern criss-crossed against the ceiling, pillars were woven with *palapalai, wawaeiole, uluhe* ferns accented with spikes of *ieie*, a form of pandanus. From the lights hung streams of red and white . . . the ranch colors.

"Long tables in adjacent rooms were set with red cloths for punch which flowed all evening . . . using up 20 cases of champagne.

"Ken Alford's Dixiecats, up from Honolulu . . . dressed in top hat, formal black suits, winged collars, continental ties, order ribbons for the occasion . . . kept the hall echoing and the party whirling and dancing until 3:00 a.m. At midnight they played 'Nani Waimea' before the string of firecrackers began their thunderous crackling that lasted for five minutes.

"Old-timers loved it when they played the old Hawaiian waltzes, 'Imi Au Ia Oe,' 'Akaka Falls,' 'Wailana,' 'Uluhua,' 'Wehiwehi Oe.' Of course there were plenty of Dixieland favorites, too. . . .

"Following beautifully-planned pre-Ball dinners over the countryside, the receiving line began to form at Kahilu at 10:00 p.m. Standing with the host was Governor William F. Quinn and Parker Ranch manager Richard Penhallow.

"With the arrival of the first guests, the note of glamour was struck. Nancy Quinn was slim in a holoku of American beauty velvet created by Elsie Krassas in Honolulu from pictures in an old fashion book of the 1880s. It had tight-fitted bodice, neckline cut low in front and softened with a ruche of Chantilly lace wired high in the back, modified mutton-leg sleeves ending in a ruffle of lace, the skirt in front hanging straight to the floor ... and in back! ... rich velvet burst into a tiered effect of bustle poufs cascading down onto the long train. Her only ornament was her mother's cameo pin.

"This party had its Hawaiian *alii*, too. In the past it might have been Kalakaua or Liliuokalani, Likelike or Leleiohoku ... maybe the lovely Kaiulani ... Prince David Kawananakoa and the Princess whose mother, Mrs. James Campbell, married Sam Parker.

"Saturday night it was Mrs. Sam Morris ... whose husband is a descendant of the ranch founder John Palmer Parker, and who as Liliuokalani Kawananakoa might have been Queen of Hawaii had it remained a monarchy. She was very elegant in a creation also by Elsie Krassas. Three-quarter length white fox covered her holoku of deep, royal-blue velvet cut with *V* neckline in front and back, finished with a soft fold of velvet that fell from the shoulders to be caught in front by a diamond and sapphire brooch. The gown hung straight to the floor ... draped back at the hipline extending on both sides to the center back where it was intricately folded into a large bustle-back bow. It was trimmed in royal blue ostrich tips, which looped at each side, forming a wide box pleat to the hemline ending in a short train. She carried a large matching ostrich feather fan and wore three ostrich tips in her hair.

"Many a husband must have observed to his wife that she'd be the Belle of the Ball ... and they weren't far wrong ... the honor could not have gone fairly to any one person. Such a collection of ruffles, flounces, bows and bustles, fine laces, ostrich feathers, ivory fans, tortoiseshell combs!

"Red-headed Mrs. Olive Penhallow, wife of the ranch manager, wore a quaint and dainty white holoku with *maile* leis. ... Mrs. George Mellen wore ivory-colored flowers in a coronet, her black satin holoku set off with pearls and white ermine stole. ...

"Mostly the men wore black tie . . . a few got into the period finery. Henry Damon was wearing what was reported to be Sam Parker's swallow-tailed coat. . . .

"Mr. Richards danced by with Mrs. Seymour Obermer in pearl grey satin . . . high ruff around the neckline, a stately ornament in her coiffure.

"Quaintly attired was Mrs. K. C. Isenberg who matched her apple-blossom pink dimity holoku with a picture hat and parasol. Mr. Isenberg substituted a pink for black tie.

"Names on the guest roster rang with nostaligc echoes of the past . . . many were descendants of John Palmer Parker . . . others from families which have been neighbors for generations. There were Seymour and Priscilla Shingle, Priscilla in black holoku wearing a feather neck lei that belonged to Seymour's mother . . . Robert and Coco Hind, Jamie and Queenie Dowsett, Mrs. Edward von Geldern who wore deep rose brocade with deep insert of black lace at the neckline and lace at the cuffs of the three-quarter sleeves. Bill and Betty Morris, Erma Lilly, Ralph and Emma King, Mona Hind, Leighton Hind, Robson Hind, Mrs. George Schattauer. . . .

"Holoku colors were beautiful. . . . Mrs. Robert Midkiff was in royal blue brocaded silk, Mrs. Sherwood Greenwell in blonde Oriental brocade, Mrs. Collins Metcalf in red brocade, Mrs. James Tabor was in crimson brocade, Mrs. Lowell Dillingham in champagne gown with empire line.

"Late comers kept coming . . . early goers kept leaving . . . the general crush of guests danced until early morning . . . when the sturdiest of the 1,000 guests then broke up into smaller groups to have breakfast in nearby ranch houses and talk over the excitement.

"By mid-morning yesterday . . . unbelievably, the town was back to life again. Some of the Honolulu people were breakfasting and packing to leave for the airport . . . many of them were joining Big Islanders for a picnic and day of relaxation at the Parker Ranch beach."

The ranch continues to prosper and improve. Its acreage is somewhat less today than it once was, but it is now a tighter, more efficient operation. Some Parker Ranch lands have been sold for resort and residential developments, but the production of beef cattle has not been affected. Whereas the ranch holdings once totaled more than a half million acres, the acreage has been pared down to 227,000 today. But with pen-feeding, the herd has been increased to more than 50,000 head.

Richard Smart insists that the ranch lands that have been sold were "strictly marginal." He adds, "They're completely wastelands from the standpoint of cattle raising. We could run cattle on the very best of those lands only a part of the year. ... The combination of cattle ranching and certain land developments, utilizing the strong potential of the ranch, will contribute to a very bright future for the ranch. There's as much of a future for ranching in Hawaii as there is anywhere else in the United States. I think we run very closely—in fact, we may produce a higher grade—than the mainland meat. We have a very, very critical market in Honolulu in comparison to the mainland market."

As for future development of the Parker lands, Smart hopes to preserve the small community influence in lieu of the large urban mass situations so prevalent on Oahu and on the mainland. He feels that development should be along the lines of individual and separate communities where the true Hawaiian flavor can survive and flourish. He shudders at the prospect of Kamuela/Waimea blossoming into a large, sprawling city with high-rise buildings, heavy traffic, and all the things which make for a gargantuan metropolis. He would like to see communities falling into a 10,000-or-less people bracket—and no larger.

It has been said that, despite its past record for dollar success with cattle, the ranch's greater wealth possibly lies in the direction of its sun-bathed coastline—premium resort real estate. Builders of luxury hotels are grasping for the chance to erect resorts along the white sand beaches. The Mauna Kea Hotel, built by the Rockefellers, is an example. The dramatic resort and subdivision development of the Boise Cascade Properties, Inc., at Anaehoomalu is another example. Boise Cascade is developing 25,000 acres of Parker Ranch land. A luxury hotel has been completed, and promises to be a substantial economic boon to all Hawaii. Signal Properties has also purchased coastal areas and other marginal lands adjoining the Boise Cascade area where they, too, plan recreational communities to exploit the popularity and growth of this South Kohala region.

But Richard Smart insists that, as the sixth-generation heir of John Palmer Parker, he will see that the best ranch lands will be "retained in their entirety." His attitude is predicated on his deep-seated belief that he owes this to his antecedents as well as to those who have and do work for him. He feels that the future of the Parker Ranch is synonymous with the welfare and future of all Hawaii. The development of the ranch's ranges, fern forests, seacoast, and valleys depends solely upon his own decisions.

On October 11, 1959, Richard Smart was quoted in the Honolulu *Advertiser:* "This is the future of the ranch as I see it. I've always felt I have been very fortunate in having this legacy, and coming from my Hawaiian side of the family that I have quite a responsibility to the Hawaiians that are left here. For that reason the ranch should continue to prosper and be held together as one project, to be passed on to future generations so that there will always be a Parker Ranch. If I can leave it in a better situation than when I inherited it—so much the better."

He has had many fabulous offers for his ranch, but has always turned them down. His reply to one mainland syndicate has been repeated oftentimes: "There is no price except that based on family pride and love of the land."

For the past several years, Smart has aimed at three specific goals:

(1) Heavy emphasis on increasing and improving the cattle herd.

(2) Development of the modern shopping center in Kamuela.

(3) Cooperation in developing and improving the tourist potential of North Hawaii.

In 1962 he ordered an about-face in ranching technique, shifting from a wholly pasture operation to a cow-calf operation, which meant that young steers were taken off grass and shipped to Oahu feedlots northwest of Honolulu to be fattened. The feedlots at Barber's Point (Ewa), Parker Ranch's subsidiary, the Hawaii Meat Company, accommodated some 12,000 head of cattle. All this made it possible for better than 70 percent of Parker Ranch beef to be marketed under a "U.S. Choice" label.

Calves are carefully watched to make sure that the blood trend is constantly improved. Throughout the year the routine is much the same. During the roundups the calves are separated from their mothers for dehorning, branding, earmarking, and injections of serum. They are then restored to their mothers and resume a normal life of eating, freedom, and growing for eight months. At that time they are rounded up once more and separated. This time the separation is permanent.

The calves become yearlings at the turn of the year. They are strong and big, fully capable of caring for themselves on more distant pastures. Two-year-olds now, they increase in size. Also, they are put into the finest pastures on the land; the measure develops them into beeves that will command the highest market price available.

Careful selection is made of the heifers so that the very best are added to the breeding herd. These replace the old and underdeveloped ones. The lesser heifers are held for the feeding pens, where they will be fattened rapidly for market. The local market of Hawaii gets some of this stock, but the preponderance of it is shipped to Honolulu.

No effort or expense has been spared in continual experimentation and development of the more satisfactory grasses. Small experimental plantings are made before being heavily sown on the ranges. A system of resting certain regions has been developed by moving the herds. This maneuver brings about improved coverage adequate for new herds to be moved in. On the lower and drier ranges, there are now nutritious grasses and legumes such as manienie, guinea, molasses, Natal red top, pangola, and kikuyu. In the higher regions, where there is more rainfall, succulent grazing is found in clovers, ryes, paspalums, brome, cocksfoot, Kentucky blue, and several other excellent grasses.

The cattle are transported via mammoth seagoing barges sectioned off into corrals. Tugs haul them on a schedule that allows for the cargoes to make Honolulu harbor at dawn, so that the unloading is accomplished in the cool of the morning. The animals are handled without undue heat or agitation. Nothing shears weight off cattle faster than rough handling, heat, and disturbance.

What contributes most to the extraordinary excellence and fine quality of Parker Ranch beef? It is thought that much has to do with Hawaii's even climate and rare pastureland. The rest is careful breeding and scientific administration of the ranch's departments.

Improvement is constant at Parker. A four-inch pipeline has been installed on the mountainside parallel to and higher than the one previously serving the ranch. It feeds a 400,000-gallon tank at the 7,000-foot level on Mauna Kea above Waikii, and is now feeding a three-inch line running for ten miles around the mountain at the 6,000-foot level. All this opens up regions of excellent grassland which formerly had not been usable due to lack of water.

This was just one of the moves necessitated by the decision to increase the herd for volume production. The herd has been expanded to more than 50,000 head, in lieu of the 30,000 that ranged the plains in the early 1960s. The horse herd, too, has been materially stepped up, mostly thoroughbreds. Many are sold to mainland racing stables, where they are establishing their own enviable reputations.

The Kamuela shopping center evokes architecturally the Monarchy Period, and is doing a thriving business. The Parker Ranch Headquarters emphasizes the Monarchy theme. The shops and restaurants are thriving.

But the long-range view has been maintained. Ample land adjacent to the already built-up sections has been held aside for additional shops and parking space.

Although much land has been sold and leased, much more is available both in fee and by lease for residential and resort development in this North Hawaii area. Smart has been, and continues to be, ever ready to give right-of-ways for state-built roads and highways to open up the country.

Meanwhile, he continues to keep the family museum in immaculate condition at Mana. The koa-timbered building, with its nineteenth-century furniture and portraits, is symbolic of the heritage of the past. It helps to stimulate drive to strengthen the ranch and move it into the future of Smart's North Hawaii.

Richard Smart has been constantly seeking new and more ways to better employee benefits in order to maintain an even more efficient Parker Ranch family. In December 1969 he instituted a substantial profit-sharing plan. The purpose was threefold; namely, to provide a means for career employees to accumulate sizable savings to supplement their pensions during retirement, to increase the sense of employee participation in the operation of the ranch, and, through the cooperation of employees and management, to effect necessary changes in methods of operation, increase efficiency, and eliminate wasteful practices.

The first distribution was paid on January 1, 1970, and approximated 10 percent of the basic salary of each full-time employee with over one year's service at the Parker Ranch.

Despite the fact that Smart already had an extremely liberal medical plan for all employees, he switched the plan to the Hawaii Medical Service Association, and considerable savings were reflected in the employee's paycheck. At first under Smart, one-quarter of the net income of the ranch was held to one side for medical care, for educational advantages, and for recreational facilities for all employees. The plan was carried out many decimals, with the employee's whole family entitled to free medical and hospital care. Now, effective January 1, 1970, all employees and their families were on the HMSA insurance plan, and the difference between its costs and the money previously spent by the ranch for medical and dental benefits, plus an addition for increased income tax, amounted to $35.00 per month saving per employee. The ranch made no money under the new program, but actually increased its expenses through the additional amount allowed each employee to partially offset his increased income tax liability, in the interest of looking forward to a new and even better era for everyone.

The employees also get free housing or housing allowances. If they wish to build their own homes, they are afforded the opportunity to buy land at low prices. Also, with low-interest company loans, every child of a ranch employee is guaranteed four years of higher education.

Apropos of whether or not Richard Smart's many ranch hands are loyal to him and feel they are dealt with fairly, a March 1970 incident is significant. The ever aggressive ILWU got to a few of the *paniolos* and stressed the advantages of joining its union. Despite the unusual benefits and profit-sharing programs already instituted by the Parker Ranch management over the years, some of the newer hands started saying that a "closed union shop" might be to their advantage. There were signs of dissension among Parker Ranch workers.

The upshot was that, with union pressure remaining persistent, Smart called a vote. On March 6, 1970, in a 75-to-18 vote by Parker Ranch employees, the union was turned down. Its representation simply was not wanted.

The Parker Ranch of today is a solid, lasting cattle kingdom, a monument to the courageous John Palmer Parker, one of the first men to pioneer the era of independent enterprise upon which today's state of Hawaii has been built. Beginning with him, and ending with the guardians of the present day, there has been an army of men and women who built this ranch empire. With their own sweat, brains, and faith, they carved out a lasting monument from a primitive, rugged region. They created handsome pastures from a savage land, established a dynasty of fruitful animal husbandry where there had been nothing but wildness before.

The Parker Ranch was home to them. They put their blood and heart into the building of it, the expanding of it; and their very character has been stamped into it. They are the ranch's fiber, and the fiber of the ranch becomes the people.

Epilogue ,

Shortly after this writing an additional change took place in the ranch's general makeup. Richard Smart negotiated with Rubel-Lent & Associates of Phoenix, Arizona, to take over management of the business and agricultural aspects of the Parker Ranch. To ensure total and highly personalized supervision of the cattle kingdom's operations, Gordon Lent, a partner in the management firm, moved to Kamuela to become general manager. None of the fine paternalism and good-will traditions dating back to 1837 will be lessened, but, more than ever before, the whole operation will be a working cattle ranch honed to turning a profit on beef.

Mr. Lent came in as the day-to-day engineer for the program and has operated closely with his firm, with Richard Smart, and the ranch's own staff specialists. Smart continues maintaining his involvement in both the policy setting and upper-level management decisions.

With all the impetus of the new program and all the long-range plans, cattle ranching is guaranteed a future in Hawaii. The intent is for future generations not only to reap the harvests from the revenues the ranch furnishes, but from that other more intangible value—the preservation of one of the state's most magnificent spreads of unspoiled land.

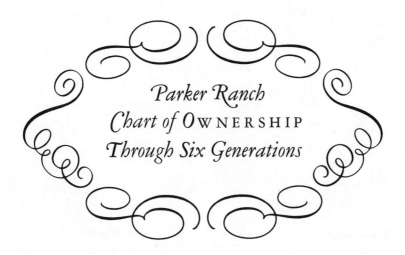

Parker Ranch
Chart of OWNERSHIP
Through Six Generations

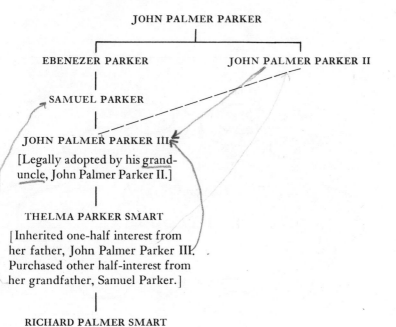

JOHN PALMER PARKER

EBENEZER PARKER   JOHN PALMER PARKER II

SAMUEL PARKER

JOHN PALMER PARKER III

[Legally adopted by his grand-
uncle, John Palmer Parker II.]

THELMA PARKER SMART

[Inherited one-half interest from
her father, John Palmer Parker III.
Purchased other half-interest from
her grandfather, Samuel Parker.]

RICHARD PALMER SMART

Kamehameha I *m*. Kaneikapolei — Kahiwa Kaneikapolei
                                  m. Kahaaulani ——————
                                  m. Namiki

The *Parker* Family
GENEALOGY

Mary P.   *m*. Fuller ———————
        m. Waipa

- Luhia
- Kaelemakule
- Kipikane   *m*. JOHN P. PARKER ———
- Ohiaku
- Honu
- Kaahiki

EBENEZER P.   *m*. Kilia ———————

JOHN P. II   *m*. Hanai ———————

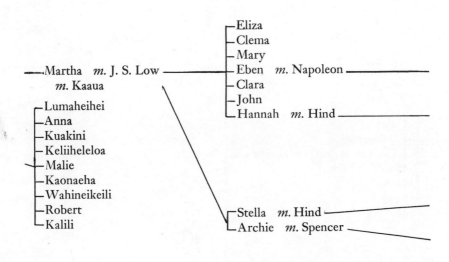

Martha *m.* J. S. Low
   m. Kaaua

- Lumaheihei
- Anna
- Kuakini
- Keliiheleloa
- Malie
- Kaonaeha
- Wahineikeili
- Robert
- Kalili

- Eliza
- Clema
- Mary
- Eben *m.* Napoleon
- Clara
- John
- Hannah *m.* Hind

- Stella *m.* Hind
- Archie *m.* Spencer

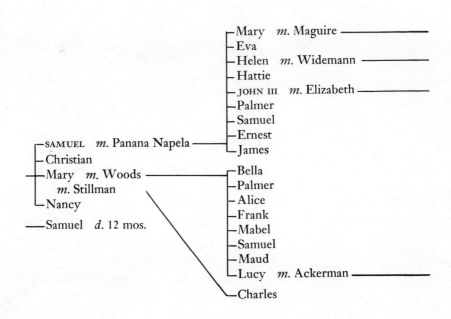

- SAMUEL *m.* Panana Napela
- Christian
- Mary *m.* Woods
   m. Stillman
- Nancy

- Samuel *d.* 12 mos.

- Mary *m.* Maguire
- Eva
- Helen *m.* Widemann
- Hattie
- JOHN III *m.* Elizabeth
- Palmer
- Samuel
- Ernest
- James

- Bella
- Palmer
- Alice
- Frank
- Mabel
- Samuel
- Maud
- Lucy *m.* Ackerman

- Charles

- Sandford
- Anabelle
- E. Woods
- Carol
- E. Jessamin
- Fuller
- Laura
- John
- Sandford

- Leighton
- Margaret
- Mona
- Irma
- Robson

- Eva
- Maud
- James

- Archie
- Edward
- Jack
- Samuel
- Stella
- Aileen   *m.* Stillman
  - Thelma
  - Mary
  - Nancy
- Parker   *m.* Hettie
  - Samuel
  - *m.* Marguerite
  - Parker
- THELMA   *m.* Henry Smart
  - Panana
  - RICHARD

- Lucille
- Pat
- Maude
- Alice
- Mary J.
- James J.

Index